THE TRAIL OF
PAINTED PONIES

THE TRAIL OF PAINTED PONIES ™

SCOTTSDALE • ARIZONA

Cover Art: Lori Musil, Yellowman, Ellen Sokoloff
Cover Photography: Eduardo Fuss
Cover Design: Evelio Mattos

This book was conceived and produced by:
The Trail of Painted Ponies, 15679 N. 83rd. Way   Ste. 4
Scottsdale. AZ 85260
Phone: 480-459-5700   Fax: 480-3615342

Visit our website at: www.TrailofPaintedPonies.com

Layout and Design:
Jean-Louis Husson, Karlynn Keyes, Rod Barker and Evelio Mattos

ISBN 0 - 9760319-0-6

Library of Congress Cataloguing-in Publication Data available

Printed in China

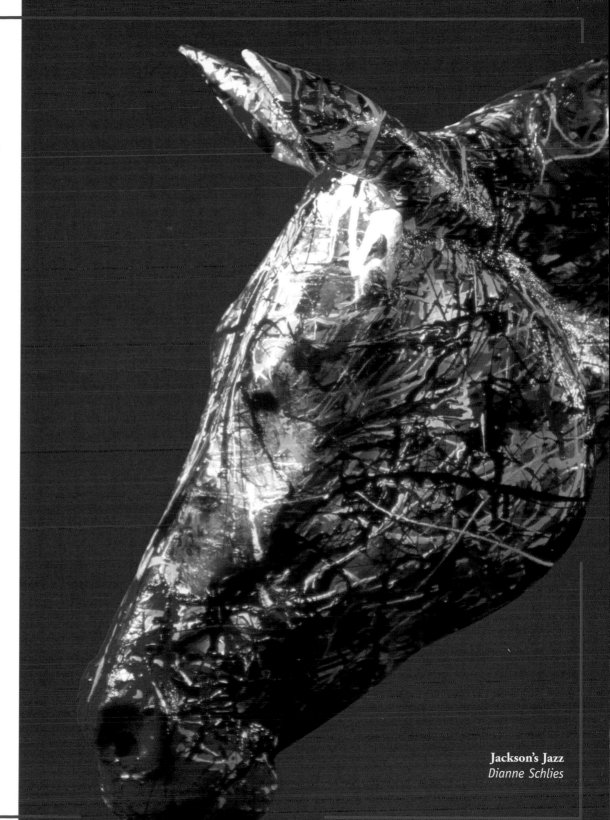

Contents

4   From the Director

5   **Horses Throughout History**

9   **Artists at Work**

17   **Homage to the Masters**

21   **Native American Ponies**

37   **Dream Horses**

45   **Music Horses**

49   **Young at Heart Ponies**

55   **Animal Kingdom**

61   **Sea Horses**

65   **Spanish Horses**

71   **Landscape Ponies**

77   **Southwestern Ponies**

83   **Patriotic Ponies**

87   **Western Horses**

91   **Racehorses**

95   **Horse Power**

99   **Maverick Horses**

109   **Pony Expressionism**

110   Facts & Figurines

114   Figurine Collection

118   Photo Finish

120   Artists Directory

122   Acknowledgements

Jackson's Jazz
Dianne Schlies

While touring southern France some years ago, I made a point of viewing the splendid, many-colored bison, deer and horses painted on the cave walls and ceilings at Lascaux during the Ice Age. What impressed me most about these masterpieces was the thoughtful use by prehistoric painters of the reliefs and uneven surfaces: the way they used the facets of rock to complement the animal designs instead of painting a flat picture. As you will see from the photographs assembled in this Collectors Edition of The Trail of Painted Ponies, the artists who have painted a Pony have taken on a similar artistic challenge. And, like their ancestors of creativity and self-expression, produced breathtaking effects and enduring art.

What began in Santa Fe, New Mexico in 2001 as a public art project intended to promote cultural tourism, showcase the artistic community in the Southwest, and raise money for worthwhile philanthropic organizations, accomplished all its goals. The Trail of Painted Ponies enchanted hundreds of thousands of people, produced dazzlingly original artwork, and raised almost a million dollars for youth, arts, social, animal, and environmental organizations.

But it did not stop there. The Trail has grown into something much larger - involving artists from around the country, and generating a magical body of art that is touching people's emotions and lives so deeply and profoundly that at times it seems the Ponies are filling a void.

Something mysterious is going on. In an effort to understand it we asked collectors to put into words the joy they get from the Painted Ponies. What we heard are things like: "Quite simply, this is the best example of creativity and love of horses I have ever seen." "The Ponies let me live out experiences I have otherwise missed, and give me hope for the future."

In the way the Painted Ponies inspire all of us to think in terms of our own creative possibilities, we think that explains their popularity. We even think our inspired pairing of sculpture and painting marks the beginning of a new, purely American art movement.

With the Collectors Edition, we have rounded up between the covers of one book the magic, the mystery, the beauty that is The Trail of Painted Ponies.

Director:

Rod Barker

Horses Throughout History

The horse has been a beloved image in art from pre-historic times to the present. As a symbol of beauty, power and speed, it has no equal. The visually exciting and culturally rich works of art that have been produced by The Trail of Painted Ponies are continuing a distin-guished tradition that began with horses drawn on cave walls at Lascaux in France 20,000 years ago, horses cast in gold in ancient Egypt, horses carved in marble on the Parthenon friezes...

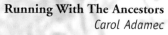

Running With The Ancestors
Carol Adamec

Out of Africa
Rhiannon Sykes

Hunting
David Wang

King Tut's Trotter
Steve Alverson

Special Gift Horse
Kay Brubaker

Olympia
Janee Hughes

The Gladiator
Carlos Machado

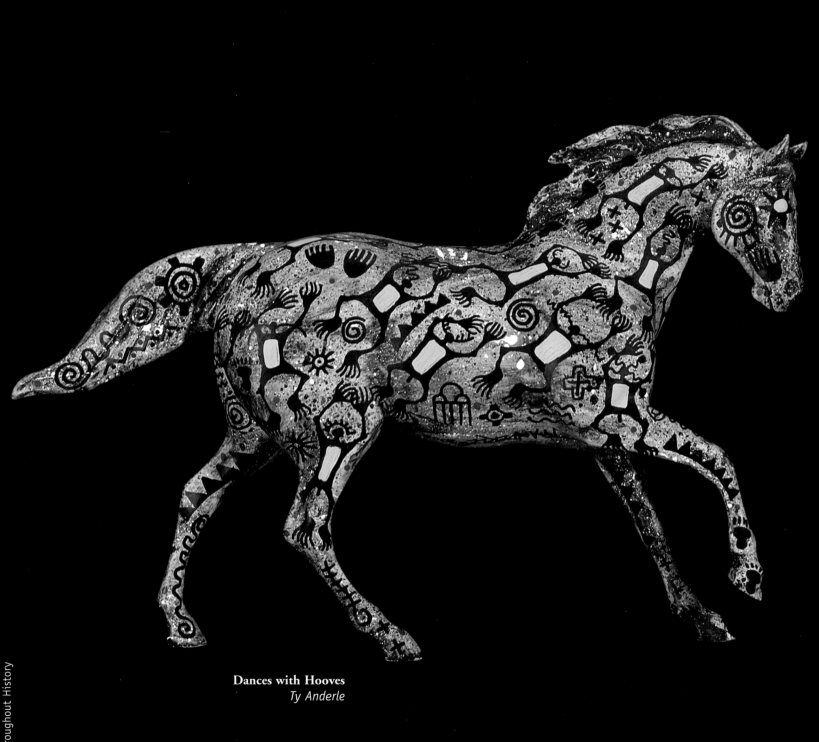

Dances with Hooves
Ty Anderle

Artists at Work

The curatorial responsibility at work with The Trail of Painted Ponies was clear from the beginning. While other "animal art projects" focused on whimsical imagery, we wanted our artwork to be distinguished by a high standard of artistic excellence.

To achieve this, certain artists were invited to participate; but at the same time a call went out across the country, encouraging unknown talents in assorted creative fields to submit designs. The results were spectacular. Inspired and motivated to produce the most challenging work of their lives, the artistic community across America responded in a way that showcased the stunningly expressive possibilities of the creative spirit.

As Long As There Is One
JD Challenger

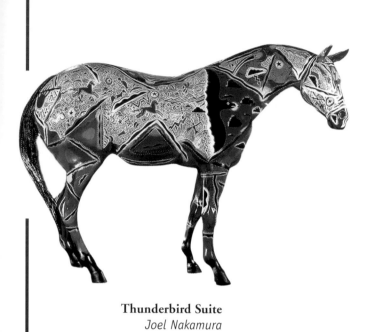

Thunderbird Suite
Joel Nakamura

Route 66 Pony
Ellen Sokoloff

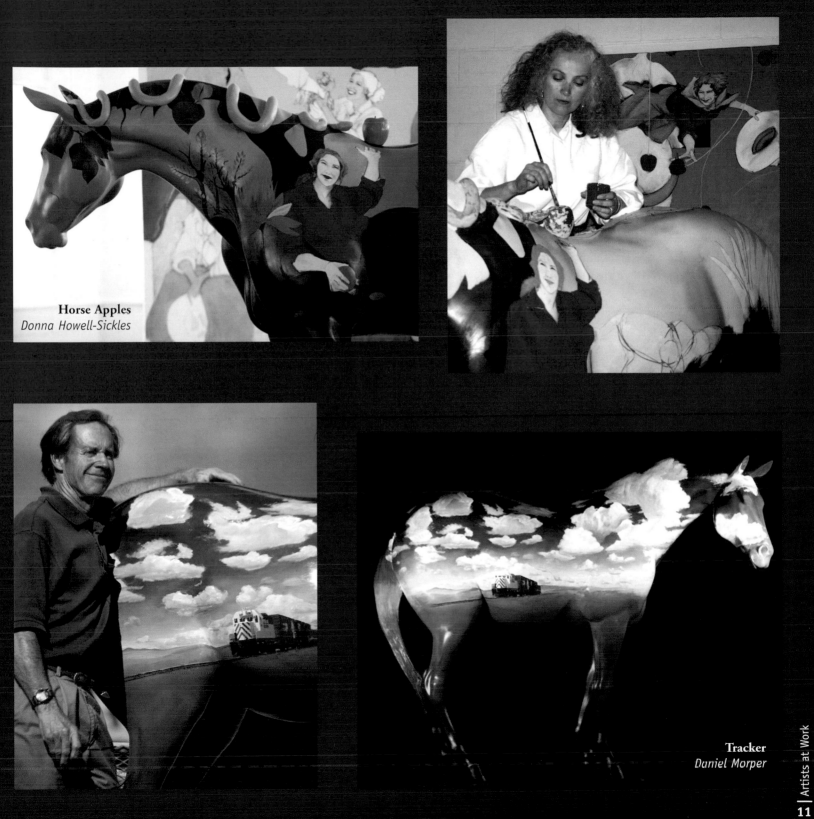

Horse Apples
Donna Howell-Sickles

Tracker
Daniel Morper

Earth, Wind & Fire
Bill Rabbit

When We Were As One
Yellowman

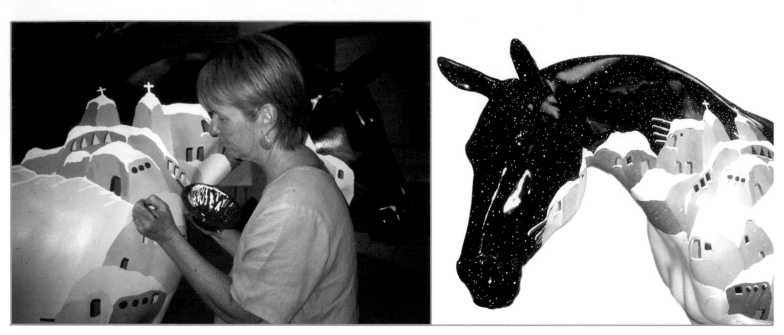

Snow Pony
BJ Briner

Karuna
Ali MacGraw

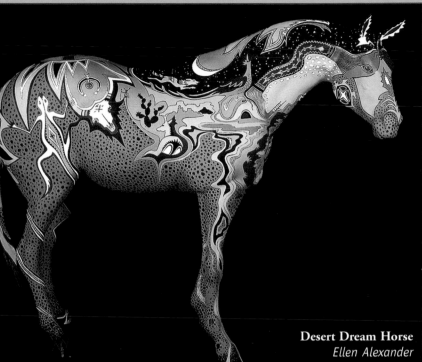

Desert Dream Horse
Ellen Alexander

Sun Magic
Storm Townsend

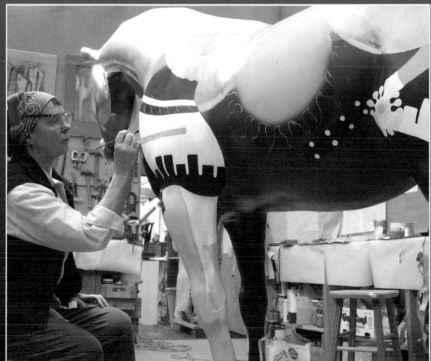

Horse Opera
Debra Tivens

Homage to the Masters

Inspiration comes from many sources. Imagining what the Masters might have created had they been given the opportunity to paint a Pony prompted artwork that evoked the style, technique and imagery of Hokusai, Degas, Van Gogh, Dali, and O'Keeffe.

Hokusai's Great Wave
Mary Sweet

Go Van Gogh
Star Liana York

Homage to Degas
Julian Robles

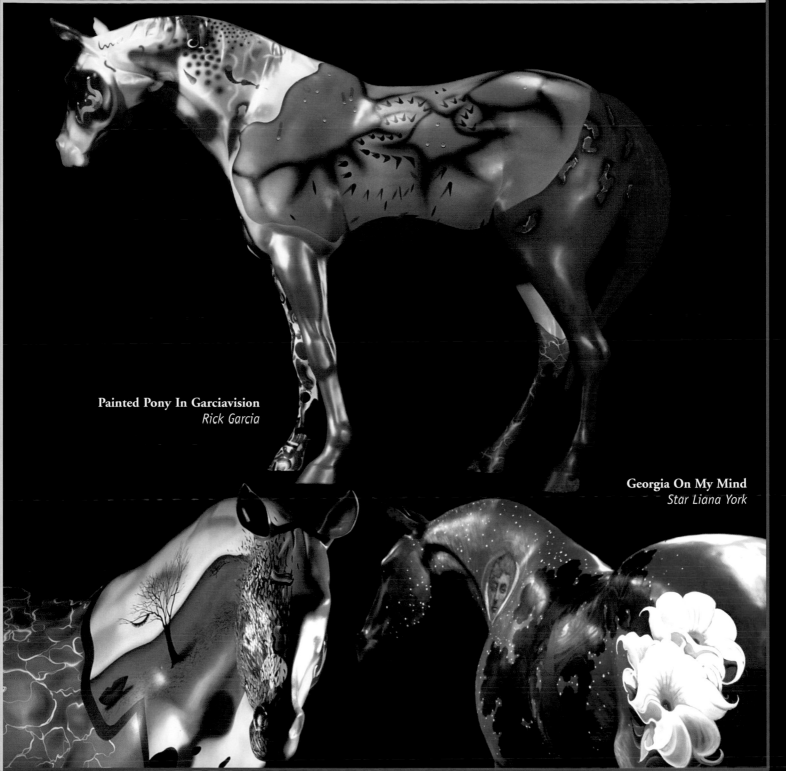

Painted Pony In Garciavision
Rick Garcia

Georgia On My Mind
Star Liana York

O'Keeffe Country
Star Liana York

Native American Ponies

There was a time when Indian art was neglected and overlooked, but not today, and not with The Trail of Painted Ponies. In recognition of the exciting and innovative contemporary Indian art that is being produced, a special effort was made to attract the most talented Native artists in America.

Artists from more than thirty different tribes welcomed the opportunity, producing a beautiful and authentic collection of artwork that carries on centuries of tradition, reveals the different cultures and societies that make up Native America, and expresses the uniquely individual touch of each artist.

The Magician
Anderson Kee, Navajo

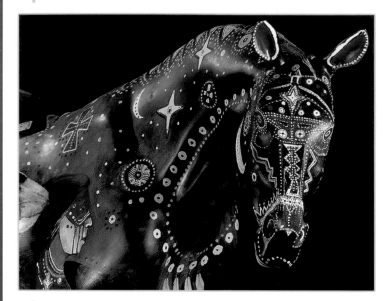

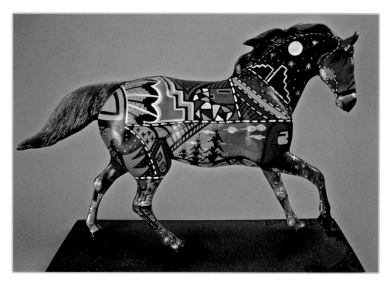

Ghost Horse
Bill Miller, Mohican

Grandfather's Journey
Buddy Tubinaghtewa, Hopi

War Horse
Rance Hood, Comanche

Caballito-Scape Con Estrellitas
Amado Pena, Yacqui

I Stand For My Horse
Beverly Blacksheep, Navajo

Crow War Pony
Kevin Red Star, Crow

Tse-Weeh-Gia-Queejo
Margarete Bagshaw-Tindel, Santa Clara Pueblo

The Swiftness of an Eagle and the Strength of a Bear
Art Menchego, Santa Ana Pueblo

Apache
Warren Sago, Apache

Horse of the Rising Sun
George Toya, Navajo

Many Horses
Michael Horse, Zuni

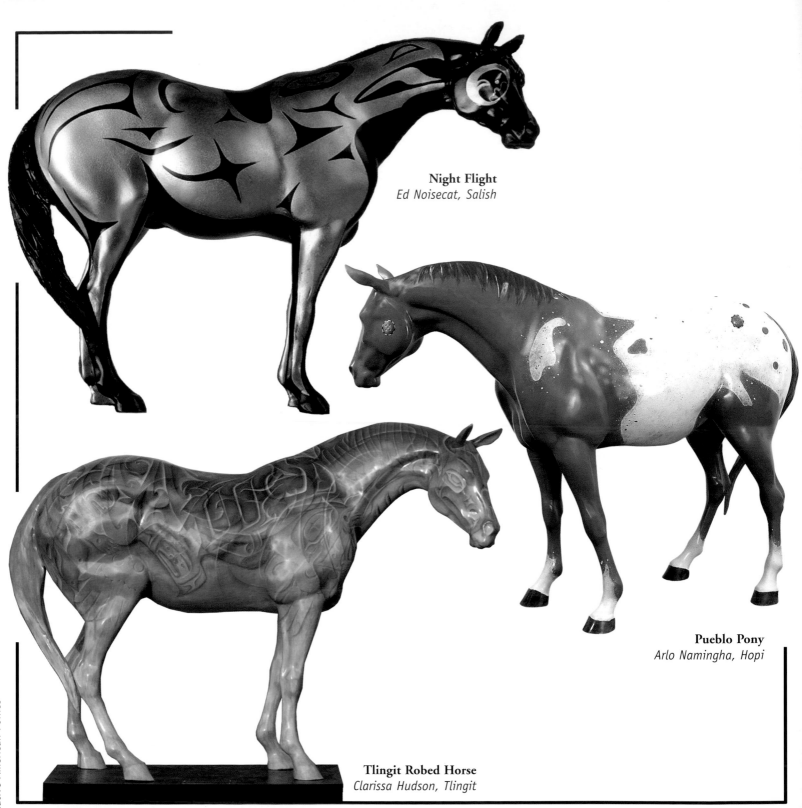

Night Flight
Ed Noisecat, Salish

Pueblo Pony
Arlo Namingha, Hopi

Tlingit Robed Horse
Clarissa Hudson, Tlingit

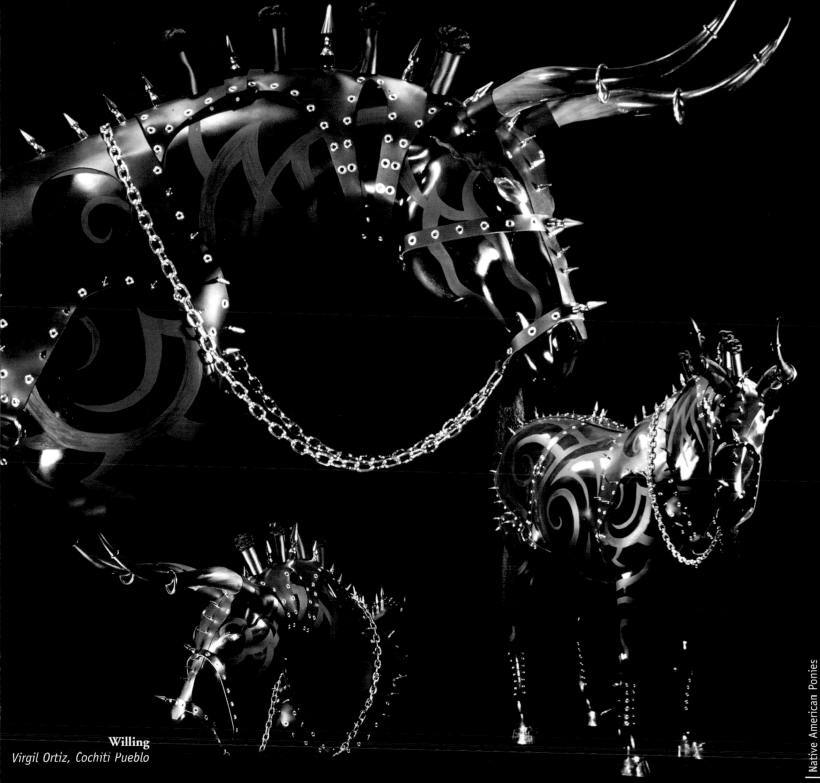

Willing
Virgil Ortiz, Cochiti Pueblo

Love as Strong as a Horse
Jesse Hummingbird, Cherokee

Tewa Pony
Tom Tapia, Tesuque Pueblo

Mad Cow Pony
Bernie Granados, Apache

Horse From The Four Directions
David K. John, Navajo

Lowrider
Romana Sakiestewa, Hopi

Blue Medicine
Mary Iron Eyes, Osage

When They Ran With Freedom
Benjamin Nelson, Navajo

Indian Summer
Buddy Tubinaghtewa, Hopi

Lightning Bolt Colt
Dyanne Strongbow, Choctaw

Dream Horses

Around the world, horses have appeared in myths as mystical representations of beauty and freedom. In the diverse hands of Painted Pony artists, they were portrayed as magical creatures capable of kicking up their heels and galloping freely across fields of dreams and fantasy.

I Dreamed I Was A Blue Horse
Joel Nakamura

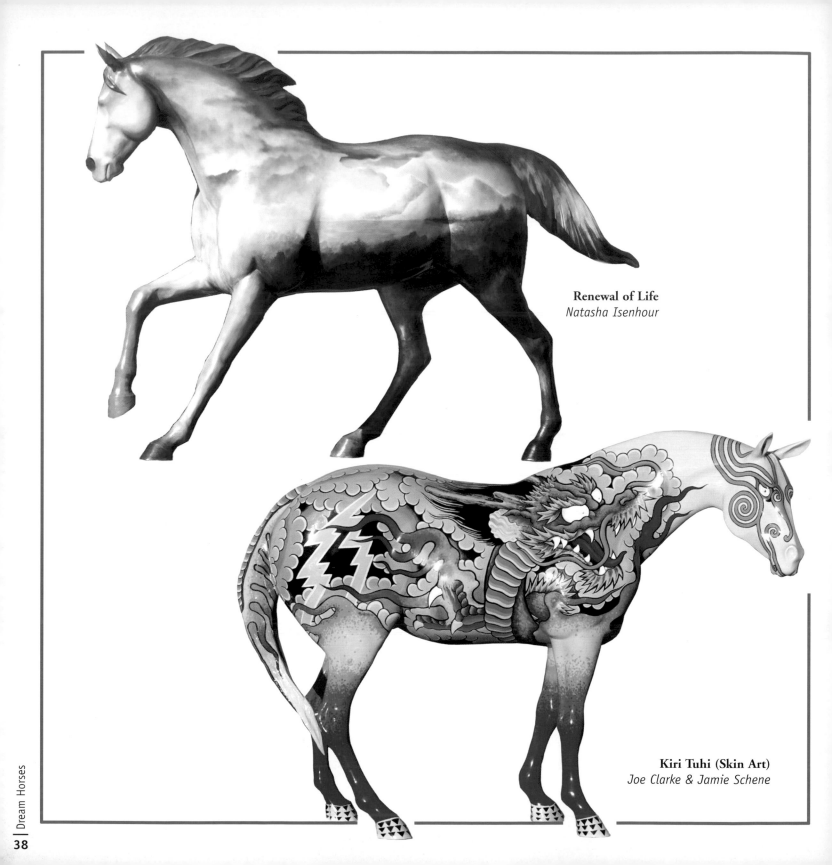

Renewal of Life
Natasha Isenhour

Kiri Tuhi (Skin Art)
Joe Clarke & Jamie Schene

Horse Feathers
Narca Moore-Craig

Three Ring Circus Pony
Kathleen Kinkopf

It's All Greek To Me
Tavlos

End of the Rainbow
Dorothea Von Eckhardt

Dream Horse
Janee Hughes

Sky Rider
Wendy Wells-Bailey

Zorse
Patricia Renk-Mayer

Silver Lining
Star Liana York

Heavenly Pony
Noel Espinoza

Sky of Enchantment
Ilsa Magener

Music Horses

From the equestrian ballets of the 17th century, when costumed horses performed intricately choreographed figures to music, to the circular parades of carousel horses whirling to the rollicking tunes of an organ, horses and music have had a colorful relationship that struck a chord in many Painted Pony artists.

Singing Cowboy Pony
Gene Dieckhoner

Jazz on a Hot Tin Roof
Kim Wiggins

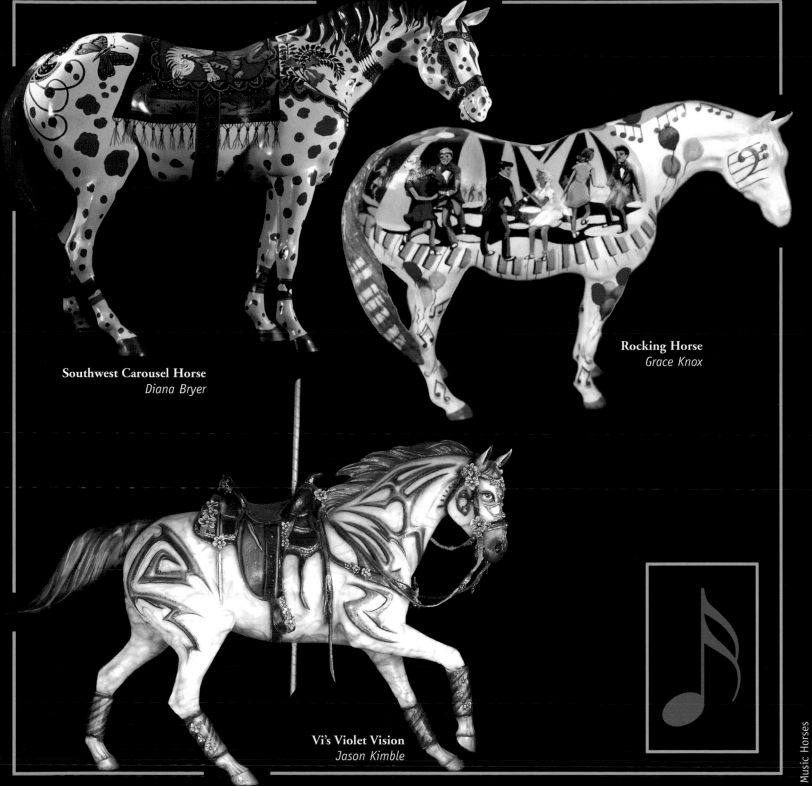

Southwest Carousel Horse
Diana Bryer

Rocking Horse
Grace Knox

Vi's Violet Vision
Jason Kimble

Kokopelli Pony
Joel Nakamura

Young at Heart Horses

For little boys it is the excitement and drama represented by knights jousting on horseback and cowboys herding cattle; for little girls it is the pageantry of horse parades and freedom of pleasure riding. The delight is the same. Horses transport youth to another world, as do those Ponies painted with a youthful spirit.

Children's Prayer Pony
The Youth of America

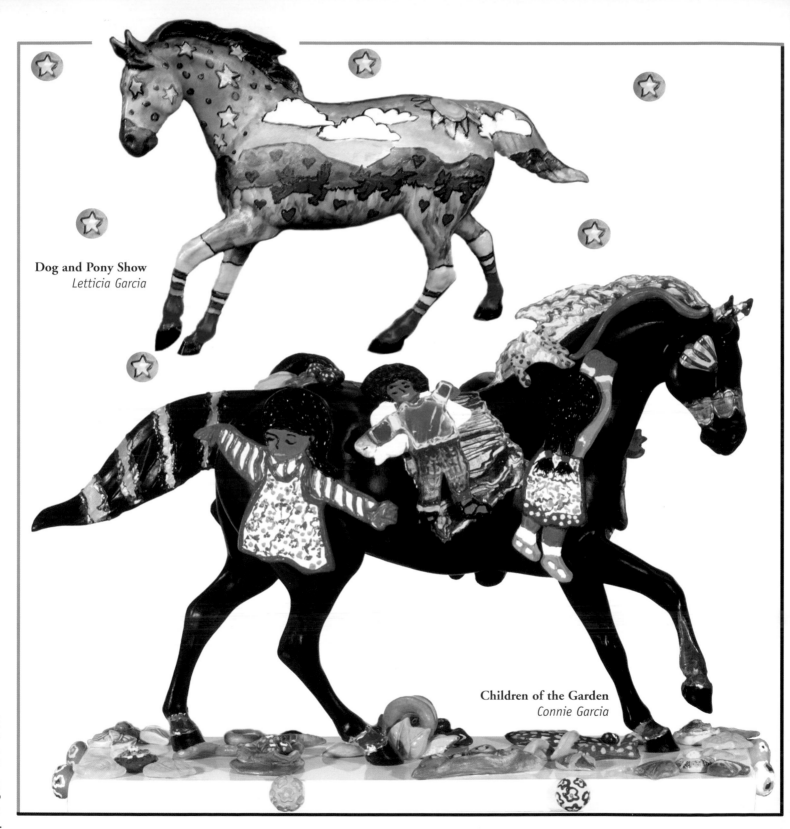

Dog and Pony Show
Letticia Garcia

Children of the Garden
Connie Garcia

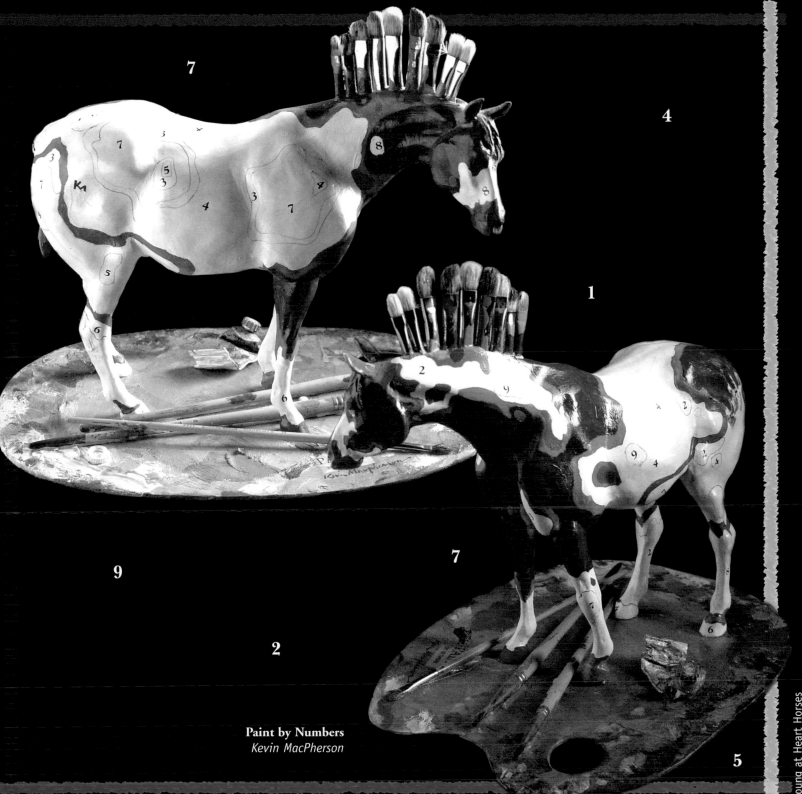

Paint by Numbers
Kevin MacPherson

Snowflake
Judith Fudenski

Nutcracker Pony
Janee Hughes

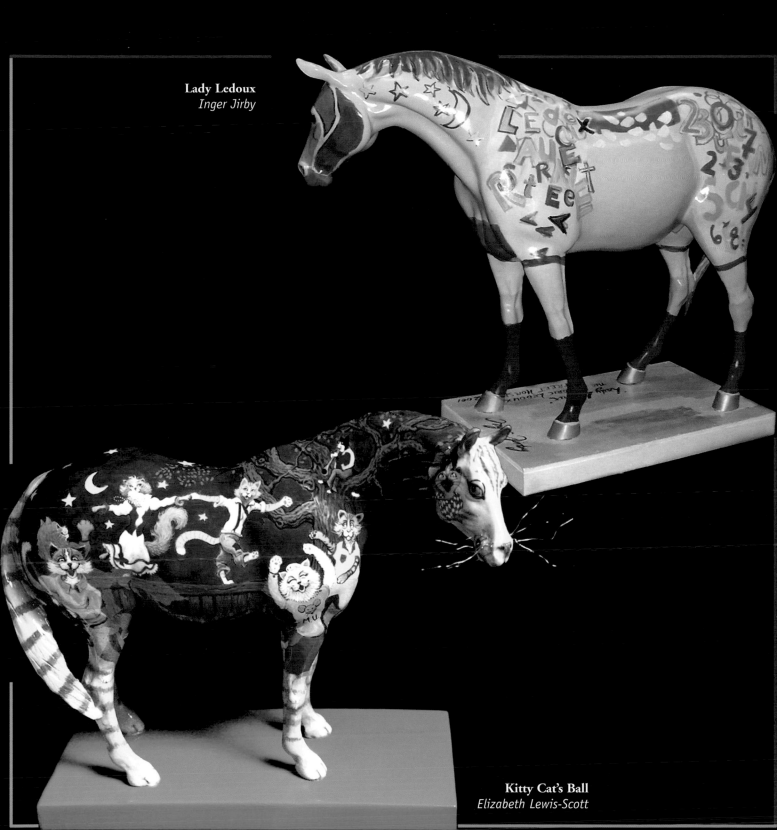

Lady Ledoux
Inger Jirby

Kitty Cat's Ball
Elizabeth Lewis-Scott

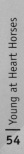

Russian Folk Tale Pony
Bonny

Animal Kingdom

The horse has always occupied a special place in the hierarchy of the animal kingdom. For many artists its stature is so exalted that it is capable of comfortably carrying the entire animal kingdom on its back.

Wilderness Roundup
Mitzi Bower

CowPony
Lori Musil

Take A Walk On The Wild Side
Gene Dieckhoner

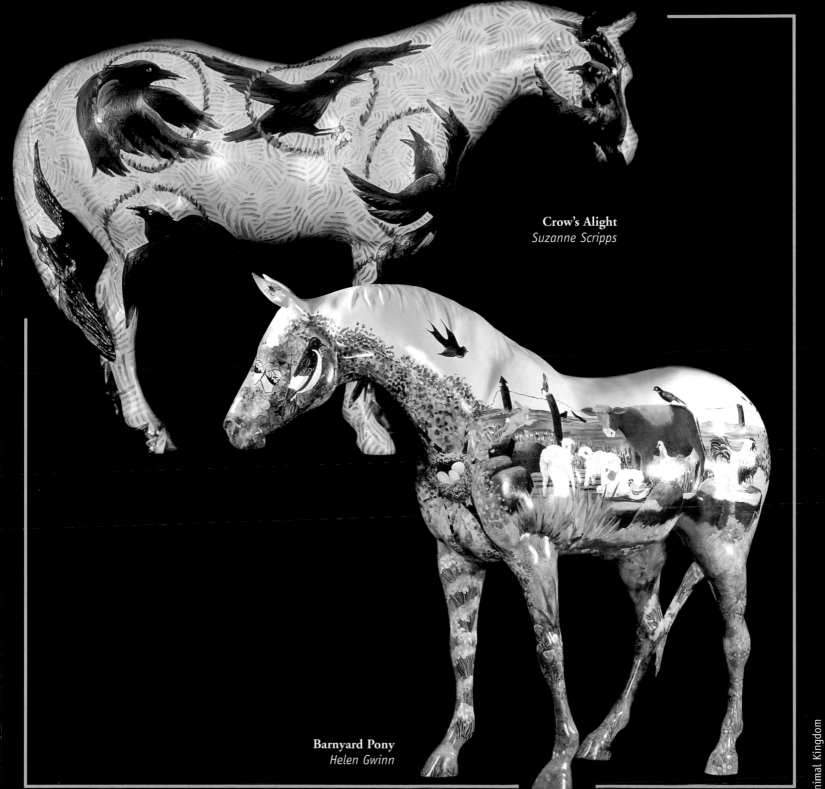

Crow's Alight
Suzanne Scripps

Barnyard Pony
Helen Gwinn

Life Rides The River
Skeeter Leard

Year of the Horse
Lori Musil

Incognito
Janee Hughes

Sea Horses

Seahorses come in an amazing variety of sizes and shapes. Thirty-five species of the ocean variety occur worldwide, and they have the ability to instantly change color, camouflaging themselves as seaweed or coral.

As for the land variety, five Ponies were painted along the seahorse theme, and they too display a chameleon-like quality. Each magically captures a different aquatic look.

Sea Horse
Grace Knox

Poseidon's Pony
Nancy Krouse-Cully

Jeremy The Fish Horse
Arlene LaDell Hayes

Tropical Reef Horse
Laurie Holman

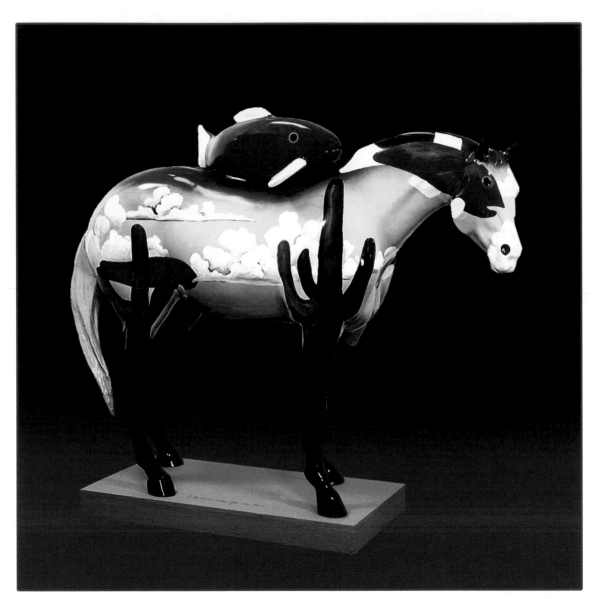

Fishback Rider
Patrick Coffaro

Spanish Horses

The horse, hunted into extinction, was reintroduced to North America in the Sixteenth Century when Spanish Conquistadors began to arrive with domesticated horses in the holds of their ships. A horse culture spread rapidly across the New World, creating a legacy that would be remembered proudly by artists of Spanish descent.

Caballo Santo
Virginia Romero

Sacred Heart
Ed Sandoval

Caballo Brillante
Roger Montoya

Maize Mustang
Pola Lopez

Milagro Pony
Connie Garcia

Sabanilla Bella
Frederico Vigil

Mesoqua Pony
Manuel Salas

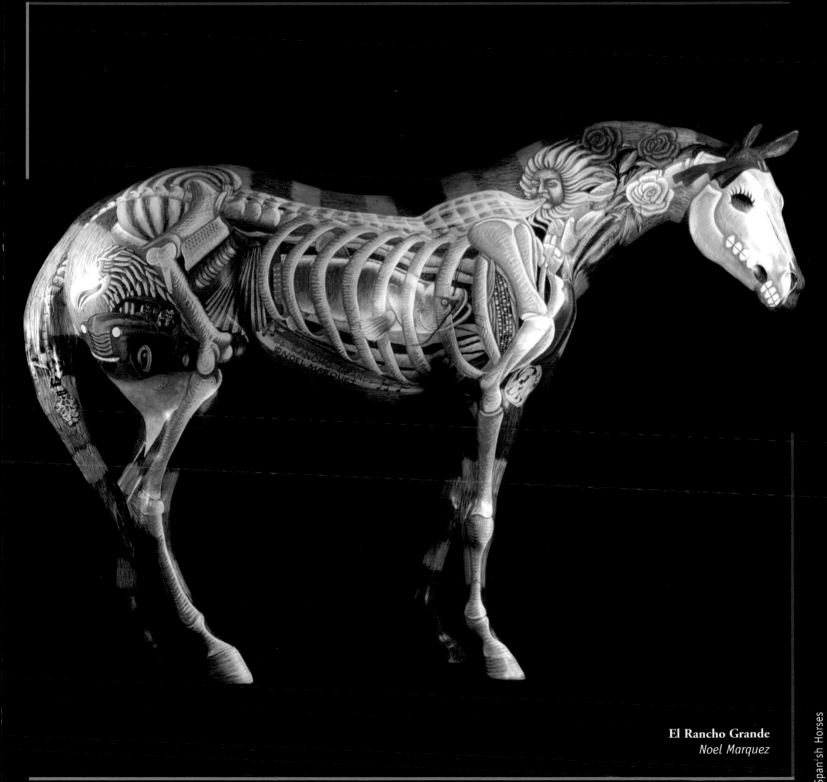

El Rancho Grande
Noel Marquez

1910
Noel Espinoza

Landscape Ponies

It was on horseback that man first traveled across the vast and beautiful American landscape. Historically, artists have shown horses as an integral feature of landscape scenes. It was a logical extension for Painted Pony artists to see the horse itself as a canvas for rendering landscapes.

Lighthorse
Lynn Vanlandingham

Your Everyday Garden Variety
Michael Campbell

Pony Tails
Fran Larsen

Night Pony
Marianne Hornbuckle

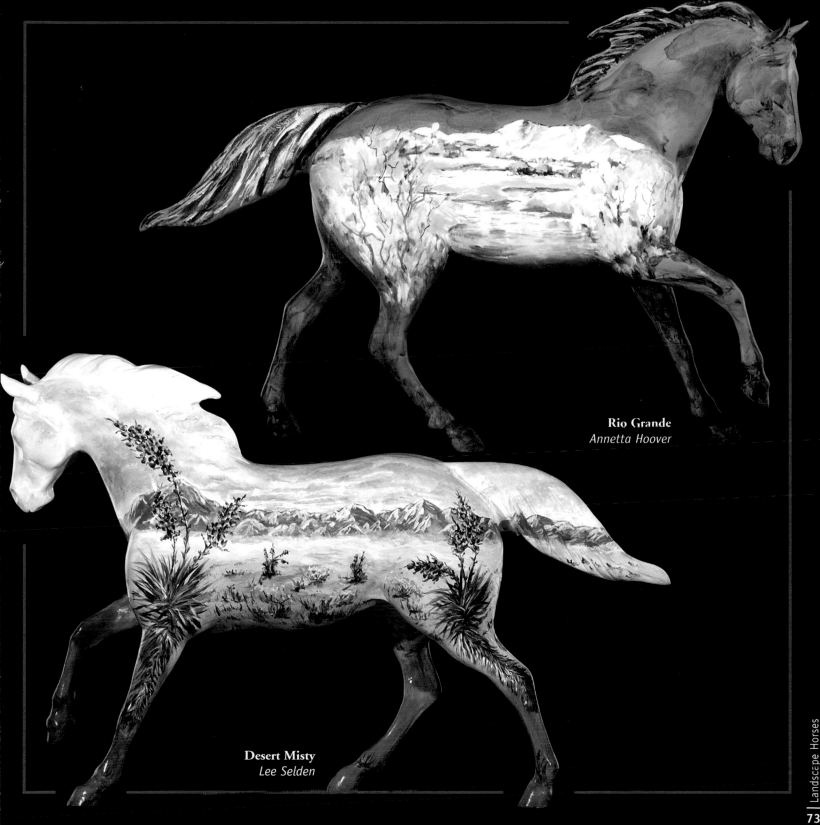

Rio Grande
Annetta Hoover

Desert Misty
Lee Selden

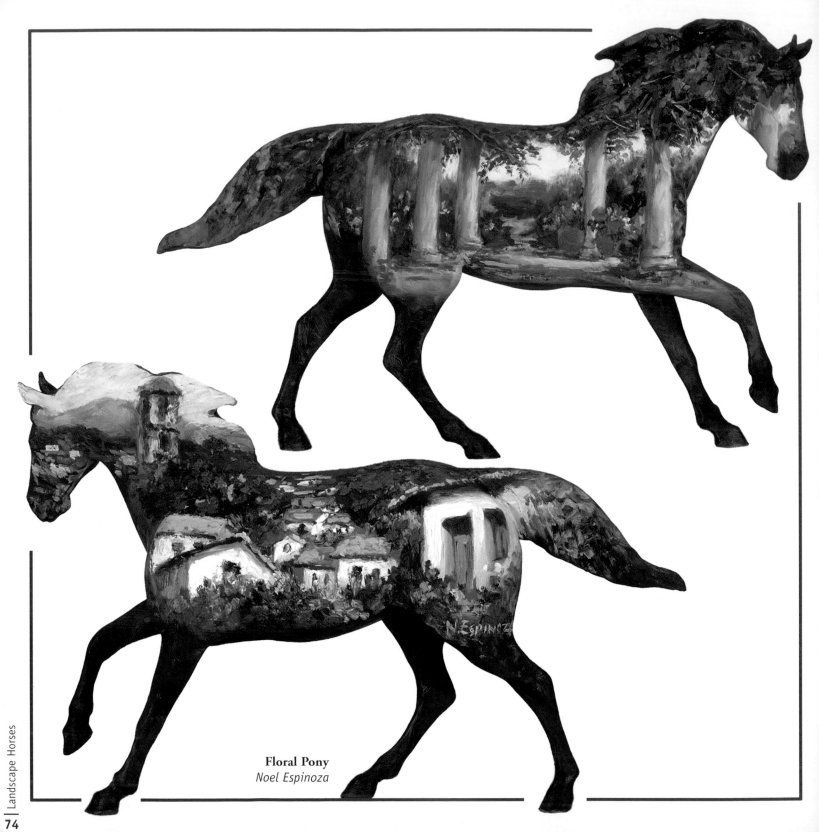

Floral Pony
Noel Espinoza

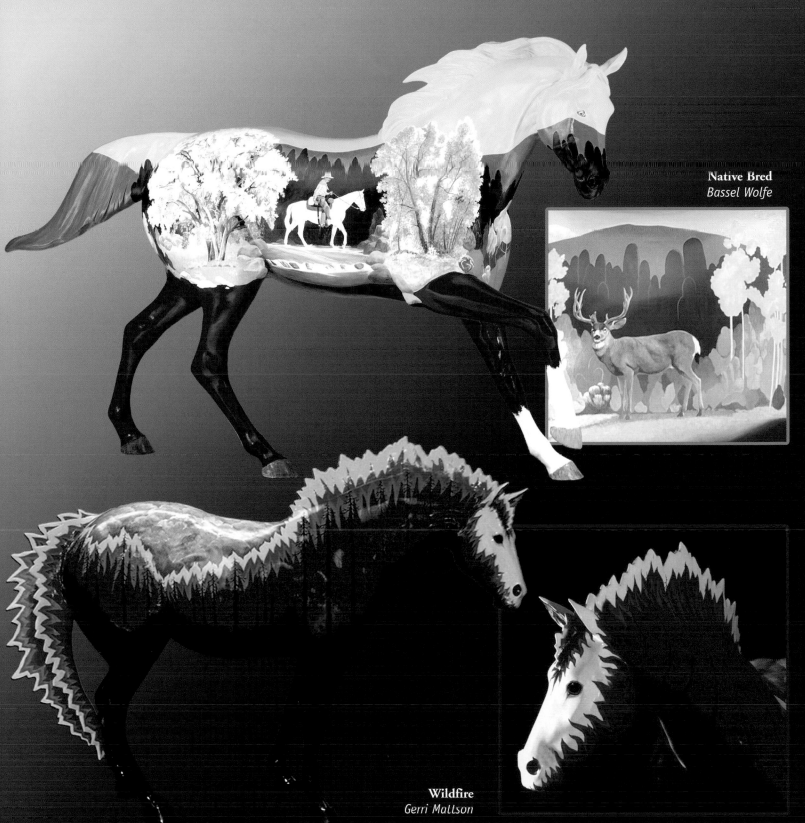

Native Bred
Bassel Wolfe

Wildfire
Gerri Mattson

Landscape Horses

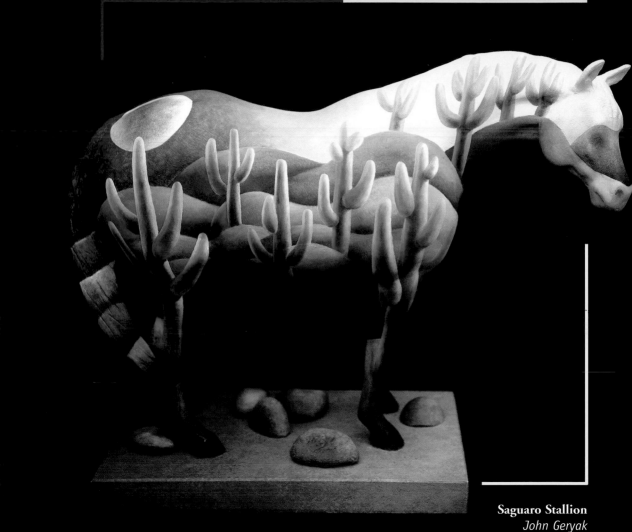

Saguaro Stallion
John Geryak

Southwestern Horses

Nostalgia for the New World conquerors, the Native Americans who became "the Lord of the Plains" once they learned to ride, the mountain men who came down from the Rocky Mountains and the cowboys who drove herds of cattle across these lands, continues to inspire many contemporary American artists.

Unity
Georges Monfils

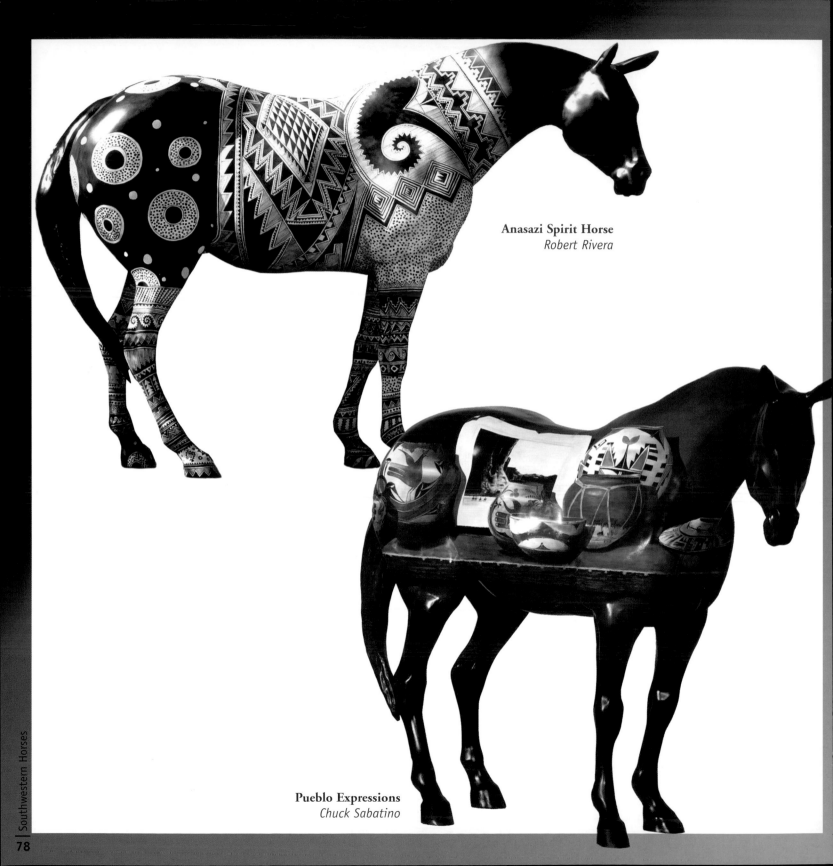

Anasazi Spirit Horse
Robert Rivera

Pueblo Expressions
Chuck Sabatino

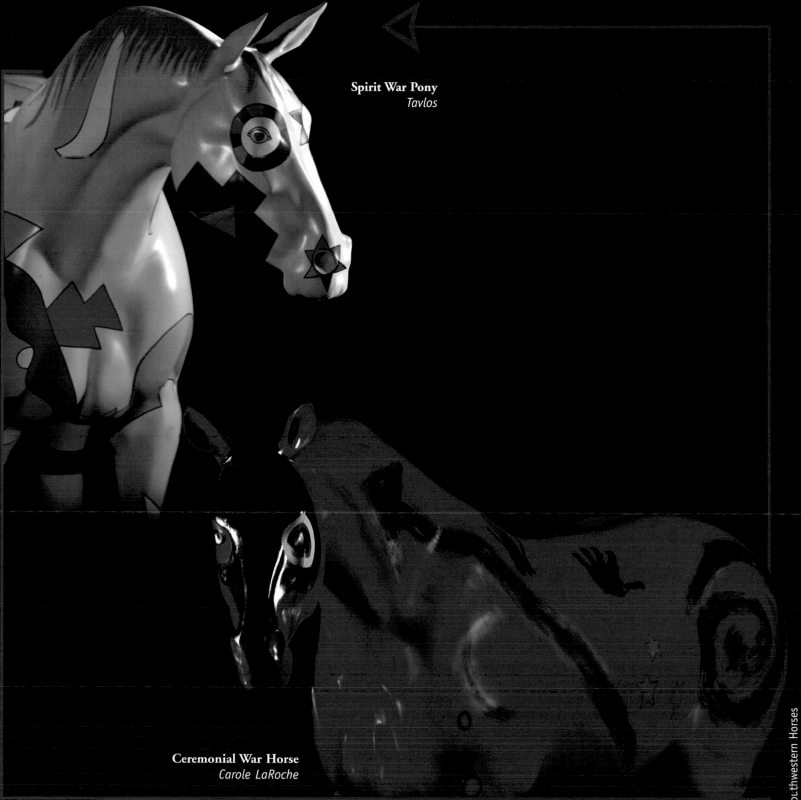

Spirit War Pony
Tavlos

Ceremonial War Horse
Carole LaRoche

Medicine Pony
Star Liana York

Horse Feathers
Loran Creech

Horsefeathers
Kathy Morrow

Storyteller
Ellen Alexander

Fetish Pony
Lynn Bean

Patriotic Ponies

As a symbol of strength and freedom, the horse is an American icon. From the historic ride of Paul Revere to the triumphs of the American Cavalry to the riderless horse that led President John F. Kennedy's funeral procession, the horse has occupied a special place in our history, and proudly represented the national spirit.

Give Me Wings
Kathy Morrow

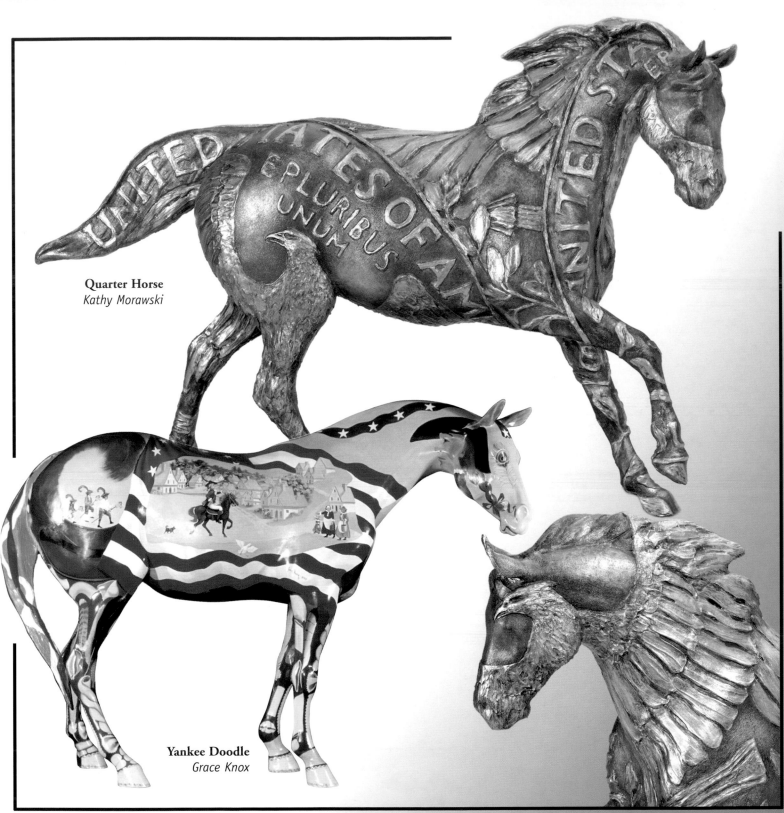

Quarter Horse
Kathy Morawski

Yankee Doodle
Grace Knox

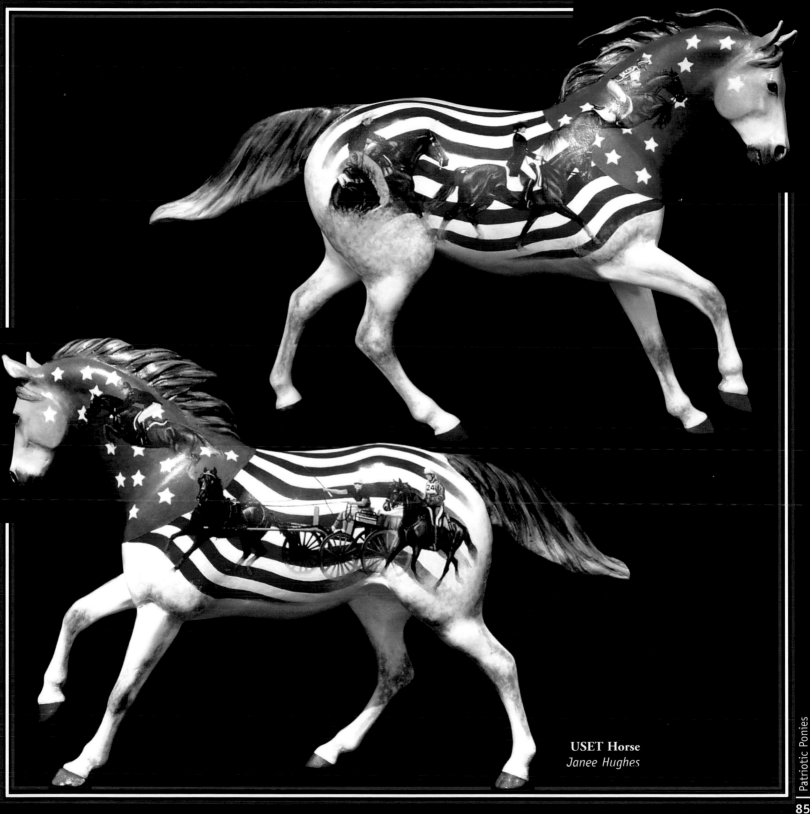

USET Horse
Janee Hughes

Fallen Heroes Memorial Pony
LD Burke, Ishmael Mena,
Shawn Pascuzzi, Bruce Hayles

Western Horses

From exploration to settlement, from ranch life to rodeos, when the tale of the American West has been told in paint there is usually a horse in the picture.

While the source of inspiration remains constant, the personal expression often takes us on a journey into an artistic frontier.

Rodeo Dreams
Jim Knauf

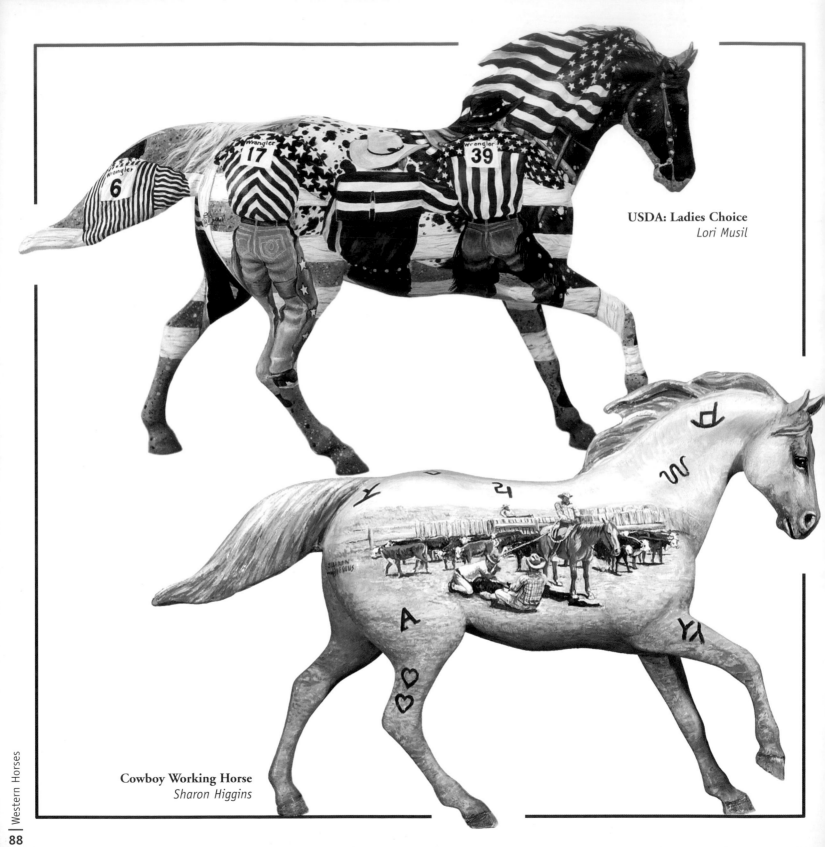

USDA: Ladies Choice
Lori Musil

Cowboy Working Horse
Sharon Higgins

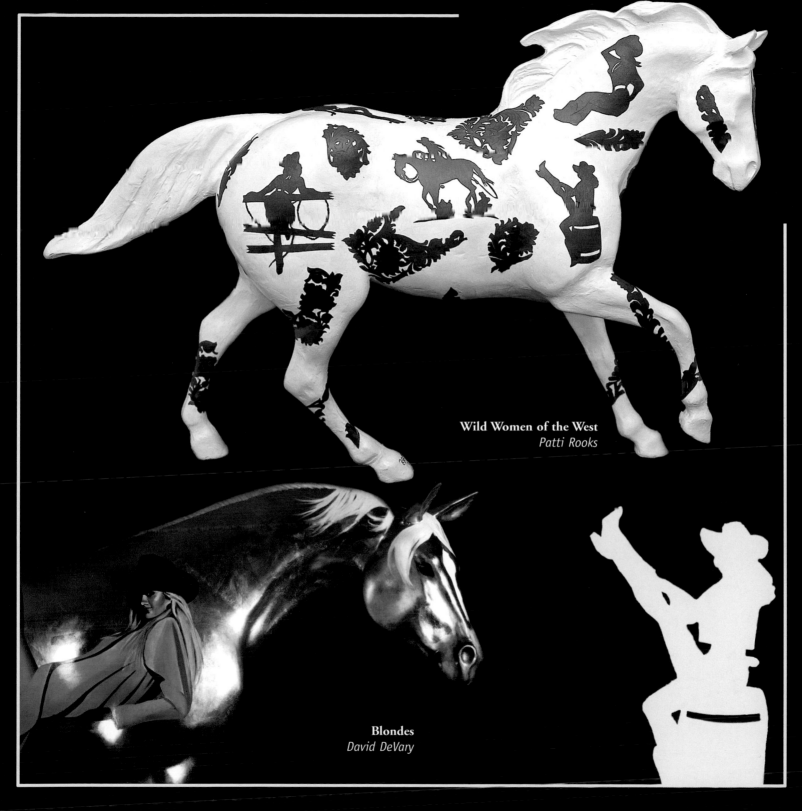

Wild Women of the West
Patti Rooks

Blondes
David DeVary

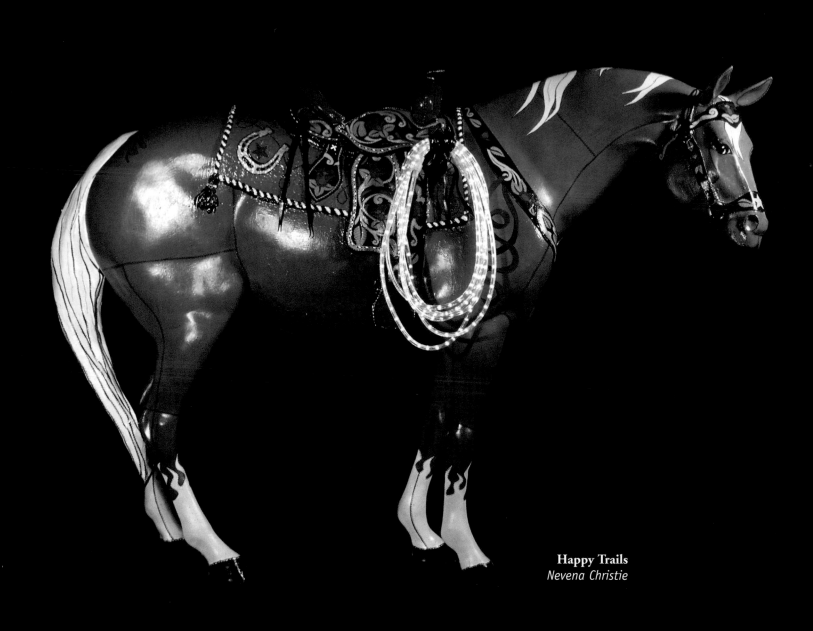

Happy Trails
Nevena Christie

Racehorses

Legs outstretched, tail and mane flowing, heads straining at the bit... images depicting the speed and power of running horses have been immortalized on canvas and in sculpture from the days in ancient Greece and Rome when chariot racing was a popular spectator sport, to the era when horseracing became "the sport of kings" and portraits of the most famous racehorses were prized, to picturesque interpretations by artists from The Trail of Painted Ponies.

Photo Finish
Janee Hughes

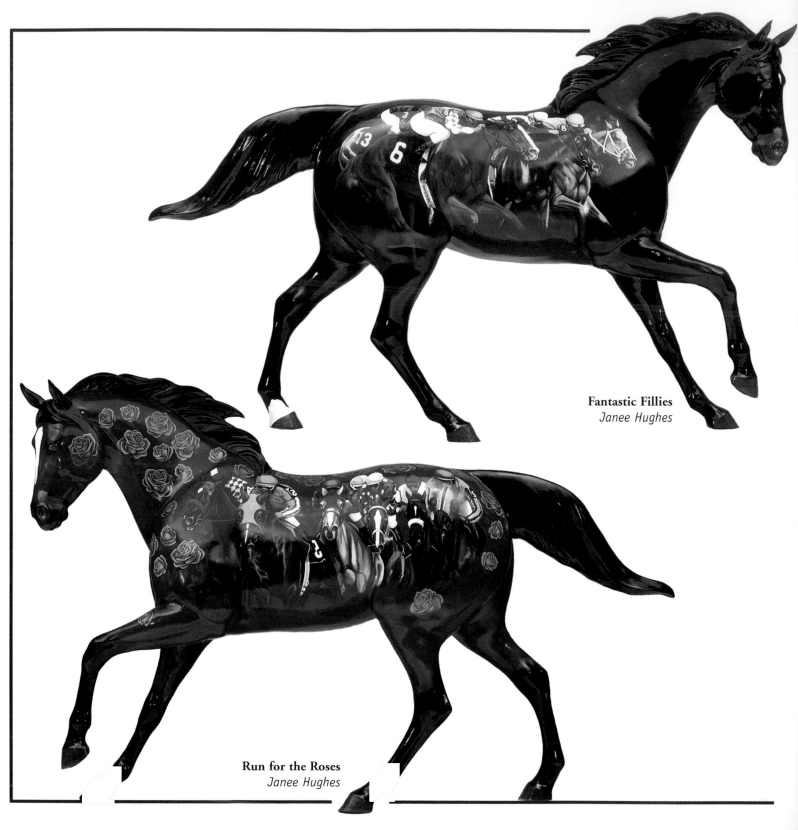

Fantastic Fillies
Janee Hughes

Run for the Roses
Janee Hughes

Race Horses
Sharon Higgins

Running Free
Luis Navarro

At Work and At Play
Laurie Holman

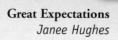

Great Expectations
Janee Hughes

Horse Power

For centuries the horse was a hardworking beast of burden, and a means of overland transportation. With the introduction of the steam engine its role in American life was diminished. But the term "horsepower" is still used to calculate the power of an engine, and horses continue to be a driving passion for artists.

Horsepower to Burn
Rich Mattson

Iron Horse
David Martin

One Horse Power
Martin Montoya

Spanish Colonial Ride
Luis Tapia

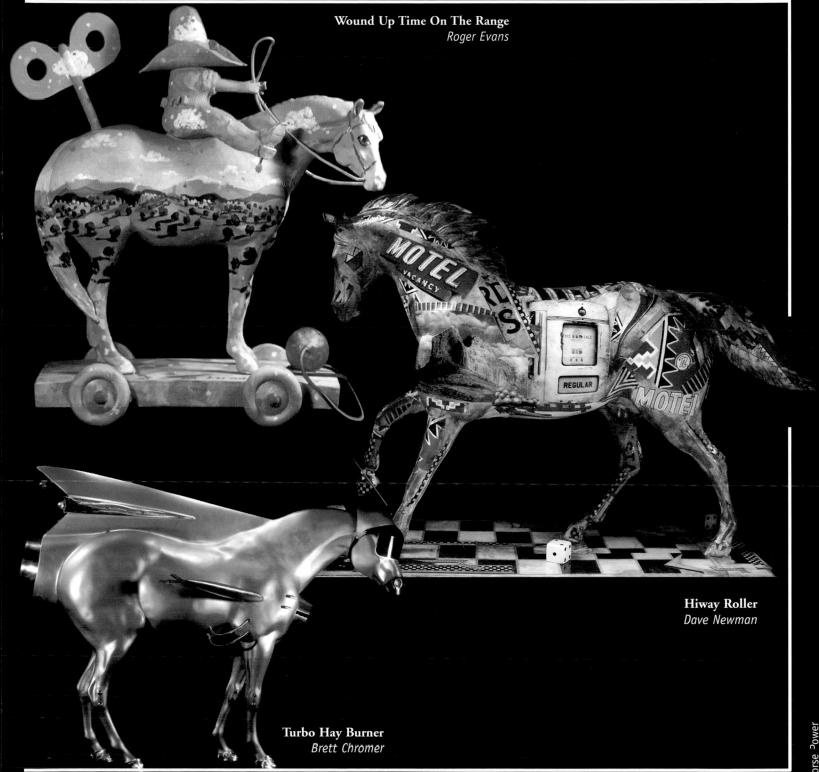

Wound Up Time On The Range
Roger Evans

Hiway Roller
Dave Newman

Turbo Hay Burner
Brett Chromer

Motorcycle Mustang
David Losoya

Maverick Ponies

And then there are the wild horses that wear no brand.... the Ponies that are painted outside the lines and are impossible to round up into a single category... yet invite us to discover their beauty and mystery.

Five Card Stud
Gerri Mattson

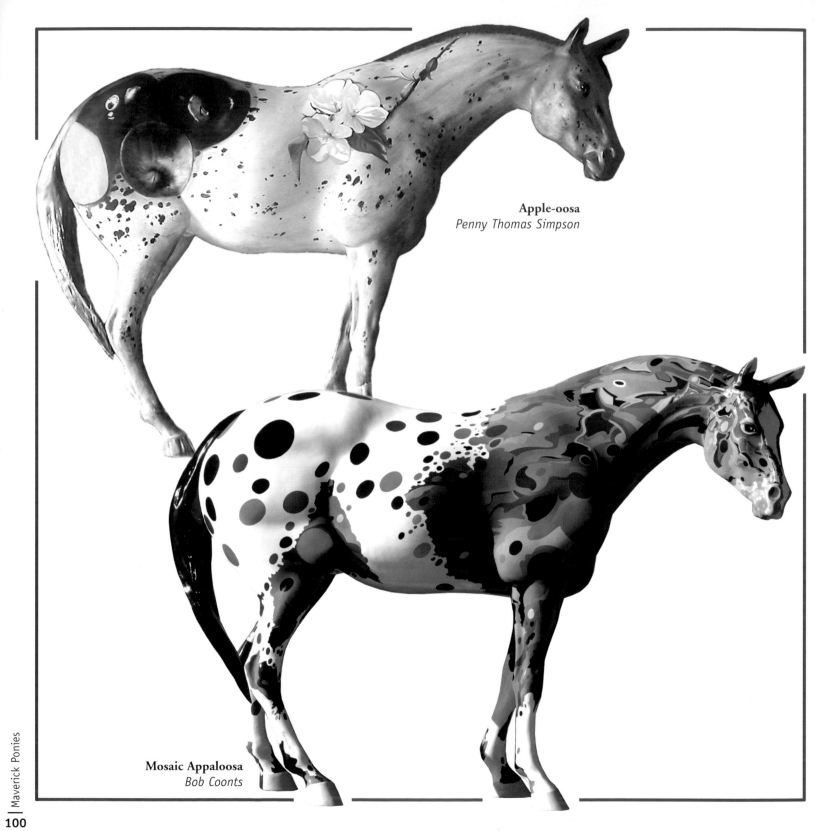

Apple-oosa
Penny Thomas Simpson

Mosaic Appaloosa
Bob Coonts

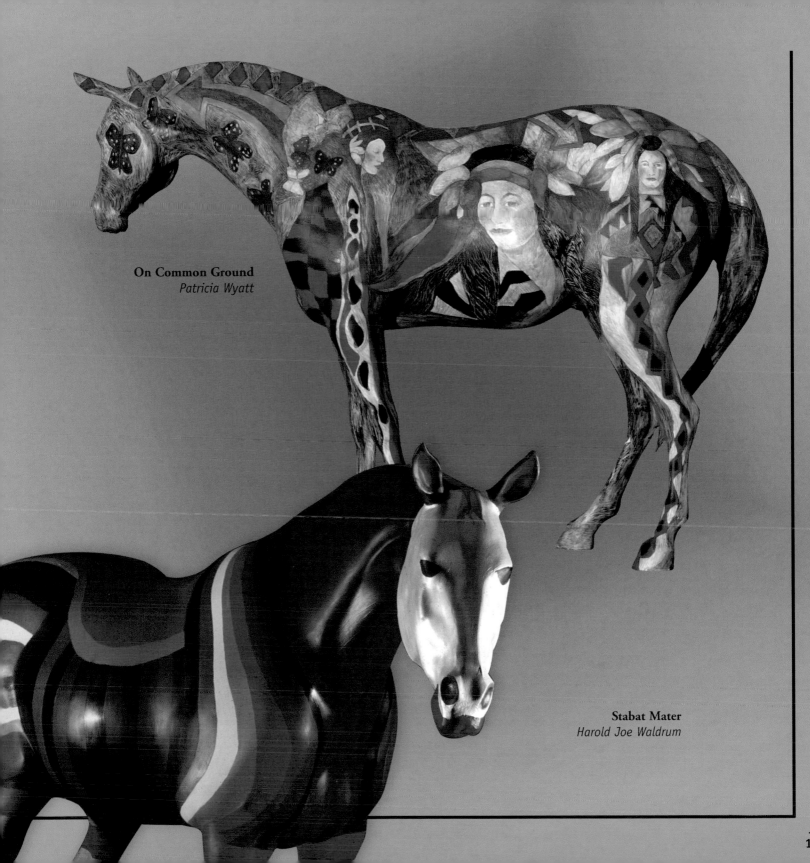

On Common Ground
Patricia Wyatt

Stabat Mater
Harold Joe Waldrum

Patrol Horse & Fireman Pony
A-1 Master Mold & Casting

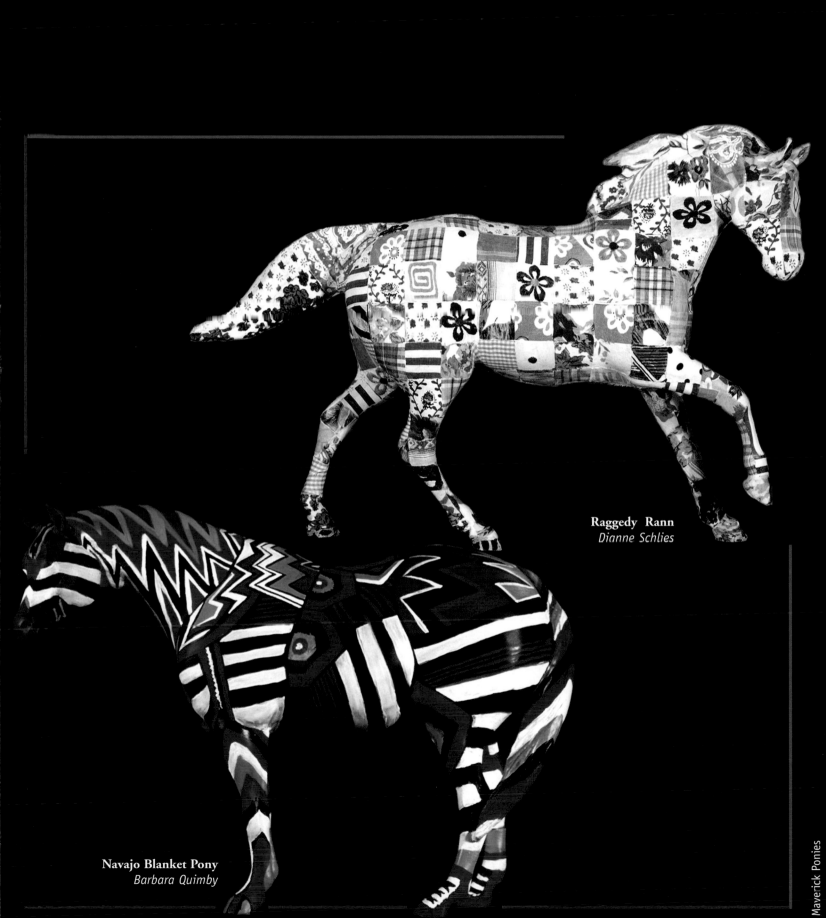

Raggedy Rann
Dianne Schlies

Navajo Blanket Pony
Barbara Quimby

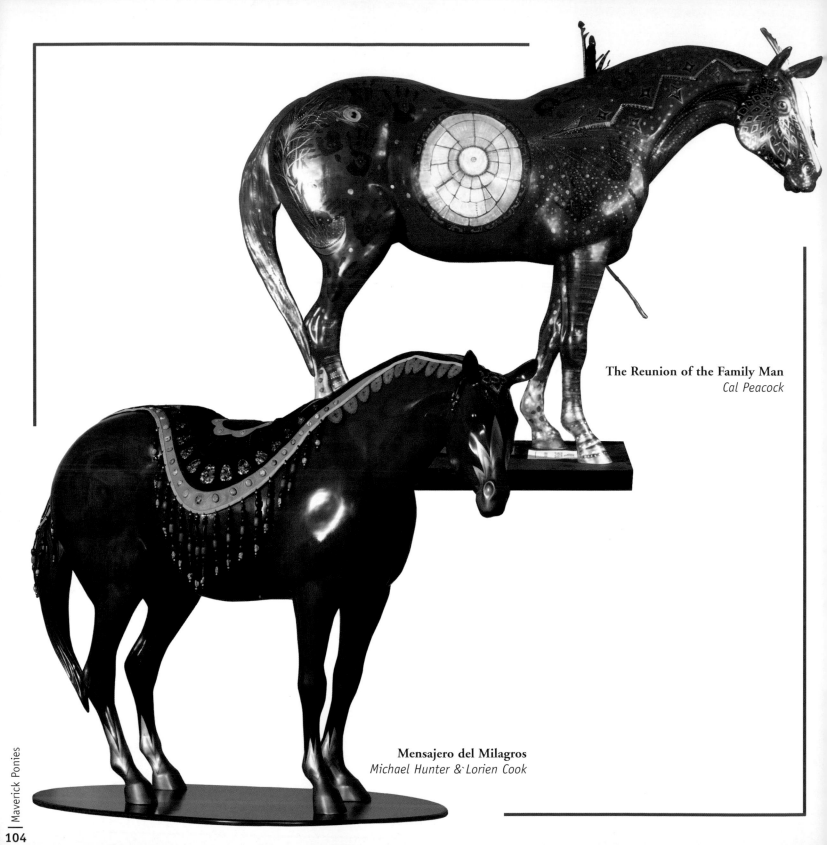

The Reunion of the Family Man
Cal Peacock

Mensajero del Milagros
Michael Hunter & Lorien Cook

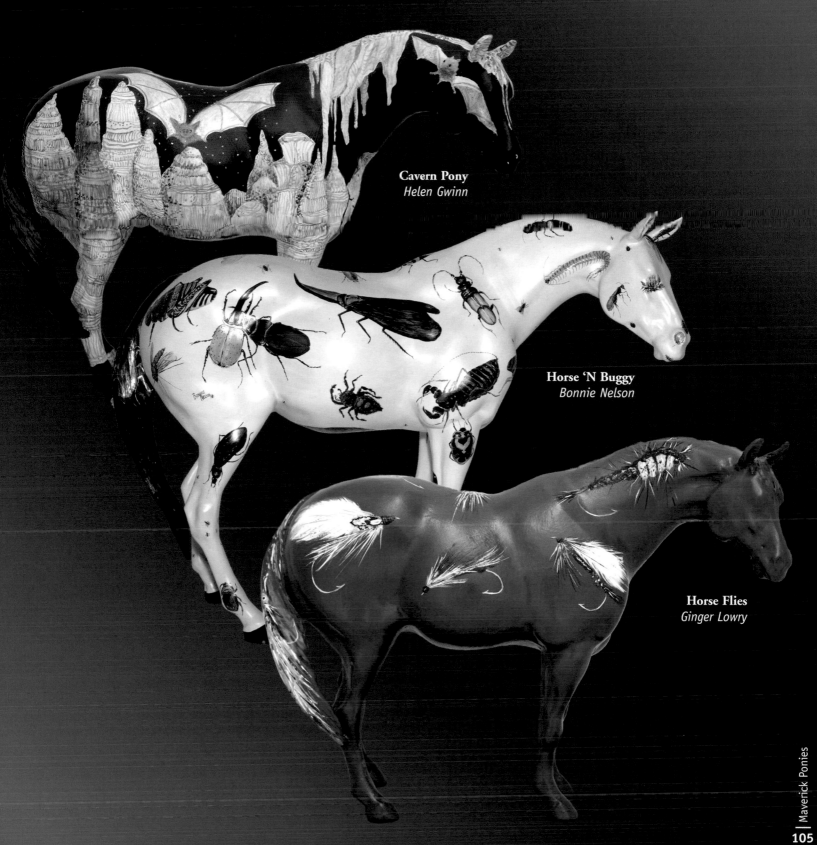

Cavern Pony
Helen Gwinn

Horse 'N Buggy
Bonnie Nelson

Horse Flies
Ginger Lowry

Caballo De Los Ojos
Anne Strait

Muy Caliente
Pat Beason

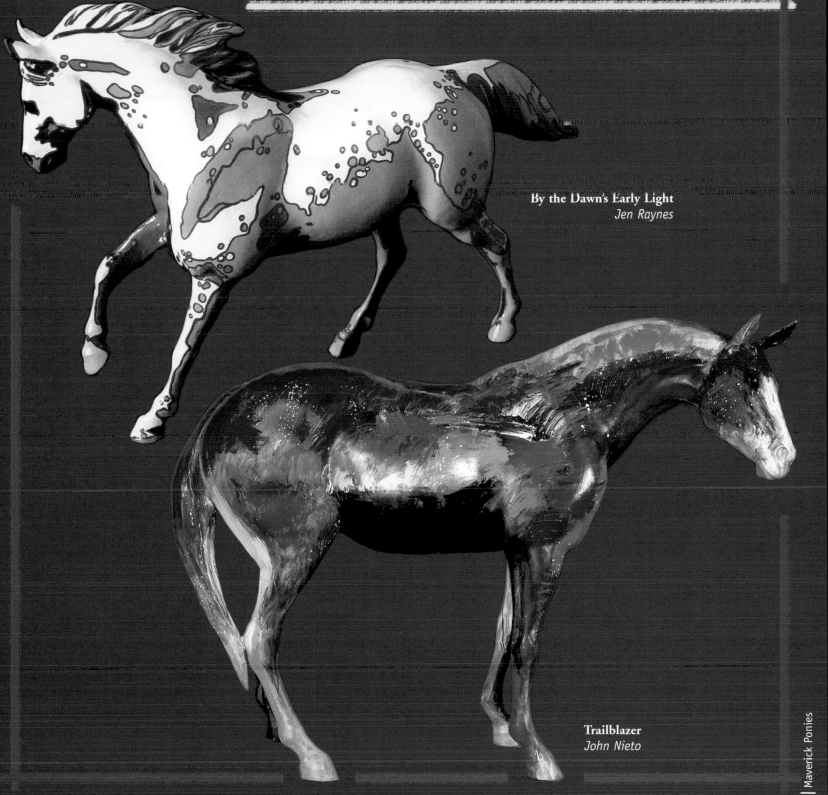

By the Dawn's Early Light
Jen Raynes

Trailblazer
John Nieto

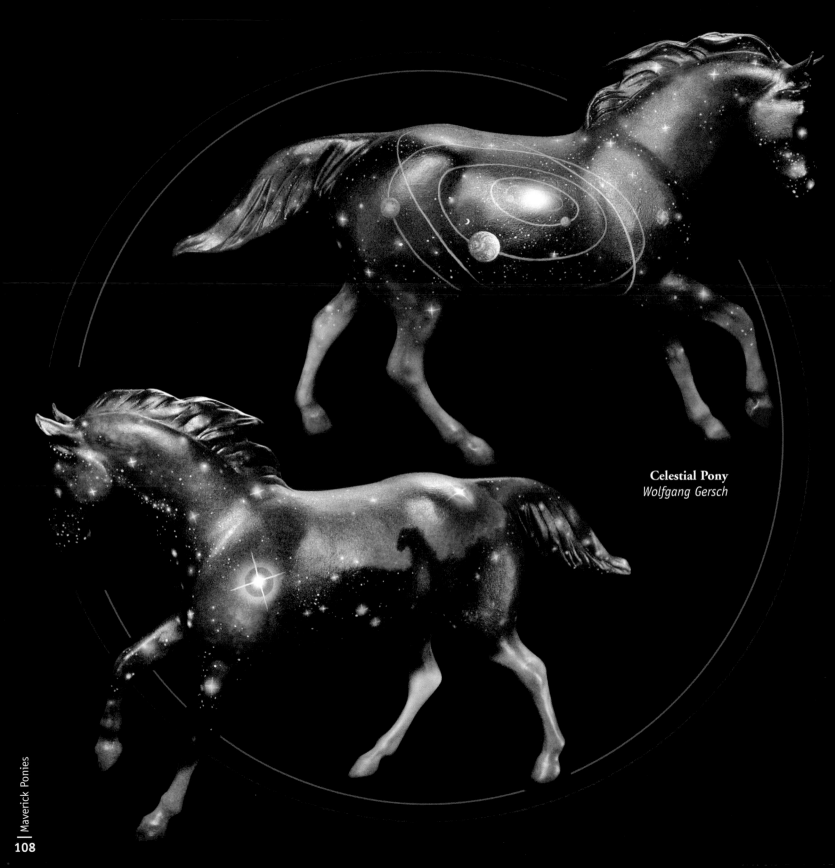

Celestial Pony
Wolfgang Gersch

Pony Expressionism

By inviting artists to explore an artistic frontier on the "canvas" of a horse, The Trail of Painted Ponies has introduced something never seen before to the contemporary art scene.

From museums to main street, reviewers are raving about the extraordinary artwork, and hailing the arrival of an exciting, new American art movement called "Pony Expressionism."

From public art exhibitions to collectible-sized figurines, The Trail of Painted Ponies is changing the way people view and collect Art.

How do you decide which Painted Pony figurines will be cast in resin and which in ceramic?

This decision is based solely on the complexity of the design. The designs that lend themselves to ceramic are those that can be transferred to the existing form with relative directness. Resin figurines, on the other hand, are usually more complex in their design, often with attachments that require sculpting by the manufacturer and the creation of a new mold. Because they cost more to produce, the resin figurines are usually priced higher than the ceramic figurines.

Are the figurines crafted as part of limited editions?

The figurines are sequentially numbered open editions. From time to time, however, we will "retire" a Pony - or, as we like to say, "put it out to pasture." This means the edition will close, and once those figurines in stock are sold, no more will be created. In the spring of 2004 we announced the retirement of seven Painted Pony figurines. In the history of collectibles, when pieces are retired their value can increase substantially.

How many Painted Pony figurines will there be?

As we can see from The Trail of Painted Ponies Collectibles that have already been created, when the imagination is given a free rein, there are no limits. We continue to invite creative minds from around the country, indeed the world, to join with us in exploring the artistic frontier through The Trail of Painted Ponies.

What other Trail of Painted Ponies merchandise is available?

At this time we have also crafted gorgeous figurine busts, lamps, plaques, coffee mugs, and coasters. Please visit us on our award-winning website for the latest information on all Trail of Painted Ponies merchandise: www.TrailofPaintedPonies.com.

Will you create other types of merchandise?

Yes. The Trail of Painted Ponies is continuing our tradition of artistic excellence as we design "lifestyle" merchandise that is original, affordable and extraordinarily well-crafted. So keep your eyes on the horizon!

Vi's Violet Vision

There are personal reasons why this artist prefers to be known by the moniker, Mister E. They are suggested in the poem he provided in place of a biography: "Adopted here, adopted there. So many names, not one my own. A father a day, not one there to stay." Though his identity remains a "mystery," his talent is evident and extraordinary. From award-winning oil portraits to comic book illustrations, with this tribute to Carousel Horses, this artist is making a new name for himself.

Artist: Mister E
Sponsor: DeVargas Mall

Mosaic Appaloosa

After distinguishing himself in the field of graphic design in Colorado, Bob established a national name for himself in the fine art field with a signature style that borders on the abstract, yet reflects a true image. "I look at animals and try to strategically place color and design elements that help define their anatomy in a different way." His paintings are part of permanent museum collections in Poland, Finland, Germany and Japan, and were displayed in special shows at the White House and Smithsonian Institution.

Artist: Bob Coonts
Sponsor: Catherine Cox

Happy Trails

A former fashion designer from New York City, Nevena wanted to create a horse that reflected the style and costumes worn by Gene Autry and Roy Rogers - '30s and '40s cowboy retro, in other words. It's no mistake that her Pony looks as if it is fashioned out of tooled leather, with a vintage saddle cinched on its back. Nevena now lives in El Paso and runs Rocketbuster Boot Company, where some of the wildest cowboy boots you will ever see are handmade.

Artist: Nevena Christi
Sponsor: Back at the Ranch

Renewal of Life

Natasha's travels abroad and around the Southwest have fueled her love for interpreting the "magical landscapes" she has witnessed. A dawn seen through mists hovering over the Rio Grande River that flows through a bird sanctuary in southern New Mexico, inspired this work of art. Whether she is painting on a canvas or a Pony, this artist has a unique ability to create a spiritual luminescence that invites the viewer to enter a meditative space that seems to live inside her art.

Artist: Natasha Isenhour
Sponsor: Socorro Chamber of Commerce

QuarterHorse

Experimenting with the design and dimensionality of an actual quarter, and the sculptural form of the horse breed that goes by the same name, this former Art Director for a national magazine found the coin's features lent themselves to the existing contours of the horse. "I particularly like how the eagle's wings flow into the horse's mane and tail," Kathy says. "By focusing on the eagle and selected words of a quarter, it also offers an opportunity to reflect an additional theme of national allegiance." A silver finish, appearing "aged" for contrast, gives the appearance of the horse a feeling of having been crafted from metal.

Artist: Kathy Morawski
Sponsor: The Trail of Painted Ponies

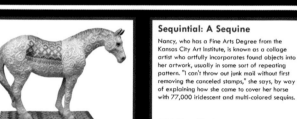

Give Me Wings

Many of the Painted Ponies carry messages or themes, and this is one for our time. It was inspired by a poem Kathy wrote after the events of September 11: "I will not forget those who sacrificed on the altar of freedom. Precious freedom, give me wings to soar beyond my dreams and touch the stars." As a child of the Southwest, the artist was raised on the San Carlos Apache Reservation and Pine Ridge Sioux Reservation, where her father trained Indian police forces.

Artist: Kathy Morrow
Sponsor: High Desert Bank

Sequintial: A Sequine

Nancy, who has a Fine Arts Degree from the Kansas City Art Institute, is known as a collage artist who artfully incorporates found objects into her artwork, usually in some sort of repeating pattern. "I can't throw out junk mail without first removing the canceled stamps," she says, by way of explaining how she came to cover her horse with 77,000 iridescent and multi-colored sequins.

Artist: Nancy Fleming
Sponsor: Minnie Wright

Rosie the Apparoosa

This work of radiant and unusual beauty was created by a New Mexico artist nationally known for using the floral form as a means for exploring the relationships of color and value in painting. Riotous displays of multi-hued roses in bud and bloom, with not a single flower repeated, sprout from earthen hooves and thorny branch-covered legs. "I dubbed her Rosie," says Marianne, "and as she departed her first stable on a warm day in May, three real rose bushes by my studio door bloomed more profusely than any past spring."

Artist: Marianne Hornbuckle
Sponsor: Santa Fe Youth Symphony

Go van Gogh

This tribute to the Dutch master, which combines two of his most recognizable paintings with a humorous rendition of his facial appearance, complete with a missing ear, was created by the sculptor who designed the actual horse forms used in The Trail of Painted Ponies art project. As talented at painting as she is at sculpting, Star, who also breeds horses on her New Mexico ranch, knows her horses, and playfully named this piece after the famous racehorse, Go Man Go.

Artist: Star Liana York
Sponsor: The Trail of Painted Ponies

Unity

It was not solely for his grand vision - combining imagery of the early Spanish explorers who brought the horse to America five centuries ago, with representations of the Native tribes whose culture was radically changed by the horse - that this former fashion photographer turned pop artist received the award for the most ambitious Pony. To give his artwork monumental impact, Georges Monfils covered it with over a million and a half tiny Indian seed beads, applied one at a time! So impressive was the outcome, which took the artist over 1,400 hours to complete, that it was nominated for the Guinness Book of World Records.

Artist: Georges Monfils
Sponsor: The Sylvia Toth Foundation

Patrol Horse

Although there is a historical relationship between horses and law enforcement - think Royal Canadian Mounted Police and Texas Rangers - the partnership today is limited primarily to search and rescue missions, and crowd control. Nevertheless, out of respect for tradition, the creative team of Dwayne & Ginger Ulibarri has created a "poster mount," smartly tacking up their Pony in an officer's uniform, polished black boots, campaign hat, mirrored shades, and the classic imperturbable expression that makes you wonder if he has eyes in the back of his head. Nothing is going to rock this Pony's world!

Artist: Dwayne and Ginger Ulibarri
Sponsor: A-1 Master Mold and Casting Services

On Common Ground

The unity and harmony of the feminine spirit resound in the vibrant art of California-raised Patricia Wyatt. As with her paintings, her Pony tells a story that speaks to the timeless themes of companionship and the collective power, wisdom and beauty of women around the world. Animals and lush flowering plants surround the figures on the artist's Pony, emblems of the natural world that pay tribute to the Earth, whose mysterious power awakens us all to life and connects all things.

Artist: Patricia Wyatt
Sponsor: The Trail of Painted Ponies

War Pony

Comanche artist Rance Hood is one of the most recognized names in Southwest Art. His paintings, known for their drama and authenticity, hang in museums and corporate collections. The opportunity to recreate a traditional war pony, complete with a buffalo pelt saddle, lance-and-shield, arrows and feathers, became the pinnacle piece of his distinguished career.

Artist: Rance Hood
Sponsor: Rance Hood Gallery

Fireman Pony

Horses were an important part of the early Fire Services, hauling water wagons to the scene of burning buildings and houses. Cleverly, and with humor and affection, Dwayne and Ginger Ulibarri have captured that sense of the horse as a fireman's best friend. As well as being artists in their own right, the Ulibarri's operate the Albuquerque foundry where the Painted Pony forms are cast.

Artist: Dwayne & Ginger Ulibarri
Sponsor: A-1 Master Mold & Casting Service

Boot Scootin' Horsey

Carla Slusher lives on a ranch in southeastern New Mexico where she paints to country-and-western music. As her vision of a dancing horse wearing a cowboy hat, jeans, and color-coordinated boots, ready for a night on the town, neared completion, it so happened that her favorite radio station played the song "Boot Scootin' Boogie." This is how she came up with the name for her Pony, which has attitude with a capital A.

Artist: Carla Slusher
Sponsor: Century 21 Associated Professionals

Caballo Brillante

Roger Montoya is a nationally recognized renaissance figure, as well known for his dance performances as his landscape paintings. He served as Artistic Director of this Pony, assembling a team of some 50 people, ranging in age from 5 to 81, from a New Mexico village to collect glass and ceramic shards from nearby riverbeds and old dumps, and arrange them into a mosaic that danced with light and color.

Artist: Roger Montoya
Sponsor: Good Hands Gallery

Karuna (Compassion, in Sanskrit)

Says actress and animal-lover Ali MacGraw, "I chose to make a fantasy creature, inspired by the fabulous horses of Central Asia, that would inspire compassion for all God's creatures, great and small, all over the world." With Karuna, which means "Compassion" in Sanskrit, Ali demonstrates that her talent and creativity extend far beyond the silver screen.

Artist: Ali MacGraw
Sponsor: Santa Fe Animal Shelter & Humane Society

Motorcycle Mustang

A second-generation lover and owner of motorcycles, David Losoya, an airbrush artist from Artesia, New Mexico, wanted to create a creature that, "If I was a biker in the 19th century, I would ride." With the help of friends and family, he molded many parts of real motorcycles onto his horse, including mufflers, a kickstarter, leather saddlebags, and chains instead of reins. This Pony rumbles!

Artist: David Losoya
Sponsor: Yates Petroleum Corporation

Route 66 Horse

Ellen Sokoloff considers herself an "Americana painter." Her artwork preserves scenes from an earlier time in our country's history. Childhood memories of western trips along historic Route 66, America's "Mother Road", inspired the collage of diners, motels, gas stations and tourist attractions that embellish her Painted Pony.

Artist: Ellen Sokoloff
Sponsor: Gulfstream Worldwide

Wildfire

Anyone who has lived in the West knows firsthand about the awesome power and unpredictability of a wildfire. As well, anyone who has ridden horses knows they too are powerful and can be unpredictable. Carlsbad artist Gerri Mattson has creatively combined these two natural forces into a single, dynamic image in which a forest fire raging out of control and horse stand together in a single artform.

Artist: Gerri Mattson
Sponsor: Randy & Meg Milligan

Navajo Blanket Pony

After receiving a degree from the Boston Museum School of Fine Art, New Englander Barbara Tomasko Quimby moved to Wagon Mound, New Mexico, where she fell in love with the native cultures and people of the West. Admiring the artistry displayed by Navajo women weaving fabulous blankets with thread on loom, she was moved to create this tribute, incorporating the color and design "of day and night, of deserts flat and mountain height."

Artist: Barbara Tomasko Quimby
Sponsor: HorsePower New Mexico

Lightning Bolt Colt

In Lakota Sioux mythology the horse is a Thunder Being who brings storms to Mother Earth. With storms come rain and change. With this in mind, Choctaw artist Dyanne Strongbow imagined a thunderstorm centered in the horse's hindquarters, breaking up as it moved toward his head into the sunny skies of a new day.

Artist: Dyanne Strongbow
Sponsor: Renee Ingold

Five Card Stud

Artistic inspiration comes in many forms. Drawing on her experience as a secondary art teacher, Carlsbad artist Gerri Mattson gave herself an assignment. She made a list of words that related to horses, and then began to sketch out corresponding ideas. The word "Stud" prompted an association with poker, which led to a horse fancifully adorned with gaming, casino, and lottery images.

Artist: Gerri Mattson
Sponsor: Dorothy Queen & The Carlsbad Foundation

Spirit War Pony

The Santa Fe artist Tavlos is credited with originating the famous howling coyote imagery that became a trademark of Southwest art in the '80s. Known for his bold colors and vivid designs, he took a pop art approach to the Native American tradition of painting their war horses, giving his Pony a turquoise coat and decorating it with dazzling accents.

Artist: Tavlos
Sponsor: Bill & Mary Lynn Oliver

Children of the Garden

This delightful creation by a "tile artist" who designs handmade tiles (www.elkabodetile.com) tells a story of children racing across a magical garden on the back of a magical horse. A place where, in the artist's words, "For a magical moment the 'real world' was not allowed to encroach." On the original Pony, the children, bugs and flowers were all formed in clay and fired for hardness before they were hand painted.

Artist: Connie Garcia
Sponsor: Jardin de los Ninos

Sky of Enchantment

After completing her studies in art, music and fashion design in Hamburg, Germany, Ilse lived in South Africa and Spain before finding paradise in the tiny New Mexico village of Magdalena. There, Ilse writes, "one is blessed with amazingly wide horizons during the day and unrivaled clear views of the stars, milky way and other galaxies at night." Adorned with gold celestial formations that sparkle with semi-precious gems, her Pony epitomizes the artist's gift for creating original and enchanting artworks.

Artist: Ilse Magener
Sponsor: None

Dances with Hooves

This Santa Fe folk artist is known for paintings and sculpture that blend Native American and aboriginal styles with a contemporary art sensibility. Ty has blanketed his Pony with intricate petroglyph and pictograph designs that seem to float on a rock-like background. "The initial impact is of a textual nature, but upon closer viewing, if one focuses on each design element as a vignette, as a picture all its own, there is much more for the viewer to explore."

Artist: Ty Anderle
Sponsor: None

Tewa Horse

Born to a family of artists and craftsmen from the Tesuque Pueblo in New Mexico, Tom (a tribal policeman) wanted to incorporate some of the traditional images that have been handed down from generation to generation, into a design that was contemporary in feeling and rich with symbolism. To do this, he combined various animal abstractions with geometric patterns. The sash represents good fortune. The blanket honors the horse as a bold and strong being. The eagle is a symbol of prosperity. The handprint stands for the loving touch of all creation.

Artist: Tom Tapia
Sponsor: The New Mexican newspaper

Blue Medicine

A gifted writer and painter, this Cherokee artist wanted her Pony to stand not only as a work of art, but an "expression of healing and support for those in need in our community." Adorned with a tribal sash made of leather, shells and beads, decorated with individual handprints of children, Mary worked overtime to complete this "vision and personal prayer" before passing to the other side in the summer of 2003.

Artist: Mary Iron Eyes
Sponsor: David Stanridge

Wound Up Time On The Range

An architect who wanted to design buildings in the Frank Lloyd Wright tradition - who wanted to work outside the lines, in other words - for many years Roger made his living as a draftsman, translating architectural designs into three-dimension illustrations. As an escape, he turned to humorous sculpture. By placing a little boy wearing a ten-gallon Stetson on the back of a Pony painted to look like a Southwestern landscape, and adding wheels to the base and a cord with a ball at the end, Roger has transformed his Painted Pony into a child's pull toy.

Artist: Roger Evans
Sponsor: The Range Cafe

Ghost Horse

A Mohican Indian from northern Wisconsin, Bill has long been one of the most admired figures in the Native American music arena. His album "Ghost Dance" brought him Artist and Album of the Year at the 2000 Native American Music Awards. As talented a painter as he is a songwriter, Bill dug deep within his music and his art to create a spiritual memorial to the massacre at Wounded Knee. With the words to "Ghost Dance" written on the horse beside the portrait of a warrior who fought the White Man but is able to overcome bitterness with faith in a better tomorrow, Bill has created a powerful and original artwork.

Artist: Bill Miller
Sponsor: The El Centro Mall

Fantastic Fillies

When she was invited to paint a Pony that honored the racehorse, Janee, a children's book illustrator, imagined four fast fillies charging down the homestretch, the winner crossing the finish line a nose ahead of the others. The artistry in her design is heightened by the contrasting colors of the horses and the silks of the jockeys set against a midnight-black background, and the determination and courage etched on the faces of the fillies.

Artist: Janee Hughes
Sponsor: Sunland Park Racetrack and Casino

Apple-oosa

Writes the artist, "This Pony has a patriotic theme without the usual red, white and blue, stars-and-stripes motif. What is more American than the apple? Hot dogs, baseball and APPLE pie... I rest my case." Working primarily in watercolors and colored pencils, Penny has won a variety of national awards for her still-life paintings - thus the exquisite realism of the apples adorning her Pony's flanks.

Artist: Penny Thomas Simpson
Sponsor: Eagle Ranch Pistachio Grove

Floral Pony

Known as a realistic impressionist, this celebrated Mexican artist whose paintings have been exhibited internationally "wanted to deliver the ambiance of the lush vegetation, the bougainvilleas and flowers of the semi-tropical region of southeast Mexico. There you can pick flowers and enjoy plentiful vegetation the year round. The people call their land, 'Eternal Spring.'"

Artist: Noel Espinoza
Sponsor: None

Love As Strong As A Horse

"It was a Cherokee tradition for each family to make and hang a mask in the house for power and protection, to keep in good luck and keep out the bad," says Cherokee artist Jesse Hummingbird, whose paintings of brightly colored, geometric faces have become his signature. "The two couples represent different seasons of life - spring and fall - and are my way of inspiring people to find soulmates with whom they can discover both the strength and beauty of love."

Artist: Jesse Hummingbird
Sponsor: None

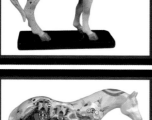

Heavenly Pony

Born in Parral, Chihuahua, Mexico, Noel has devoted his efforts as an artist to sharing a vision of Mexico as a place "as colorful and vivid as a memory." Of his inspiration for his Pony he writes, "The nobility and spirit of the Horse is so high and sublime, it led me to take them to heavenly heights in the shape of billowing clouds."

Artist: Noel Espinoza
Sponsor: None

Grandfather's Journey

As a young boy growing up on the Hopi mesas of Northern Arizona, Buddy would accompany his grandfather, a Hopi war chief, as he made his rounds on the back of a donkey checking on the corn fields and herding sheep. Years later, when he developed into a multi-talented artist collected by enthusiasts from around the world, Buddy would credit his grandfather's gift for storytelling with the imagery - Kachina figures, corn maidens, lightning storms - that found its way into his cottonwood carvings, his mystical oil paintings, and his fabulous Painted Pony.

Artist: Buddy Tubinaghtewa (Hopi)
Sponsor: The Trail of Painted Ponies

Earth, Wind and Fire

Read this Cherokee artist's resume and you will understand why he is listed in Who's Who in American Art. A Vietnam veteran whose personal philosophy is "Everything is an experiment. That goes for life, for art and for painting a Pony," Bill adorned one side of his Pony with a portrait of a Plains Indian warrior, and the other with a serene Pueblo scene. Asked for his inspiration, he wrote, "From the Great Spirit and Mother Earth, All things are made."

Artist: Bill Rabbit
Sponsor: Oasis Gift Show

Wilderness Roundup

The challenge of creating a wonderful work of art on a large scale, and not allowing her disability to limit her imagination, motivated Mary - wheelchair-bound after suffering a spinal injury during a gymnastics event at age 17 - to paint a Pony. Hoping to communicate the "... rounded up... a dazzling menagerie of animals in a changing seasonal environment." Over a year in the making, Mary's Painted Pony is an extraordinary achievement that carries this message: "Enjoy her beauty, follow your dreams, and believe in yourself."

Artist: Mitzie Bower
Sponsor: Tim and Mitzie Bower

Thunderbird Suite

Award-winning artist Joel Nakamura is known for his unique style - a blend of folk art and sophisticated iconography - and for his ability to convey stories in an intricate and engaging manner. Joel chose the Thunderbird myth for his Pony because "It was said ... enough to ride his horse under the Thunderbird's great shadow would gain sacred spiritual powers." Joel's paintings have illustrated articles in publications as diverse as Time and Playboy, and his illustrations were featured in the opening and closing programs of the 2002 Winter Olympics.

Artist: Joel Nakamura
Sponsor: Santa Fe Youth Symphony

Medicine Horse

Recognized by Southwest Art magazine as one of the top 30 artists featured in their 30 years of publication, Santa Fe sculptor Star Liana York is as well known for her detailed and sensitive renderings of Native Peoples as her gift for capturing the spirit of the horse in three-dimension. With Medicine Horse, she has combined her love and knowledge of people with special relationships to animals by creating a Plains Indian ceremonial horse dressed with a collection of personal objects believed to give the horse's owner power: shields, a lance, a bow, a pipe and assorted amulets and talismans.

Artist: Star Liana York
Sponsor: E.Stephen and Kim Charlton Benson

Golden Girl

In a serene and majestic setting among heavenly clouds, the angelic Golden Girl watches the hustle and bustle of life below... and wishes for peace on Earth. A designer at Westland Giftware, Joy is a published children's book illustrator and has also worked in the children's educational CD-ROM industry.

Artist: Joy Steuerwald
Sponsor: Westland Giftware

Kitty Cat's Ball

"Here is what happens when daytime-snoozing feline souls cut loose by the light of the new moon. They jig and waltz, slide a sinuous tango and pound out a mad polka," says Elizabeth, an avid horsewoman, Pony Club mom, and associate member of the American Academy of Equine Art from Huntsville, Alabama. "By day, we only see those half-smiles on snoring kitty faces as they grace our chairs and sofas, or doze in the garden beneath the lilacs. They grin from within as they recall the gavotte from the night before and shiver with delight, dreaming of the next Kitty Cat's Ball."

Artist: Elizabeth Lewis Scott
Sponsor: The Trail of Painted Ponies

Christmas Clydesdale

Imagine a Christmas sled full of laughing children being pulled down a snowy city street by a massive but reliable draft horse festively adorned with a holly wreath... and you have the inspiration for this Christmas Pony. Mike, the Art Director at Westland Giftware, has been a designer in the industry for over 25 years. Joy is a designer and Product Development Coordinator at Westland.

Artist: Mike Dowdall and Joy Steuerwald
Sponsor: Westland Giftware

Anasazi Spirit Horse

The intricate black-and-white designs found on Anasazi pottery at Chaco Canyon, which reflect the timeless character of ancient cultures, are the inspiration behind this astounding work of art. Of French and Spanish descent, Robert has also added new dimensions to the art of gourd painting, for which he is respected and collected worldwide. A versatile artist, his horizons are constantly expanding, making him one of the most exciting talents working today.

Artist: Robert Rivera
Sponsor: Private

Snowflake

Remembering Christmas eve snowfalls at her grandparent's lake cottage, watching big lazy flakes drift through the night sky and "dreaming of the pony that Santa would surely bring this year," moved this professional musician and bookstore owner from Sunnyside, Washington, to create this new Christmas classic.

Artist: Judith Fudenski
Sponsor: None

Children's Prayer Pony

In times of great distress, it seems that many Americans turn to prayer, one of the oldest and simplest forms of communication, and truly one of the most powerful and inspiring. In the fall of 2001, at a time when this country was changed forever, children of many faiths from across the United States were invited to share their most prized possessions - their prayers. The compassion, courage, hope and forgiveness they expressed in words and art were collected in a bestselling book - Children's Prayers for America - and are shared on this special, heartfelt Pony that is an expression of hope in its most humble form.

Artist: Youth of America
Sponsor: Pope John XXIII and Double Star Studio

Nutcracker Pony

Drawing on imagery from the 19th century Russian ballet, "The Nutcracker", Janee, a former art teacher from Salem, Oregon, has created a strikingly original and theatrical tribute to this Christmas tradition, as perfect in detail as a Faberge egg. The Nutcracker Pony is about magic and music and family and celebration.

Artist: Janee Hughes
Sponsor: None

PHOTO

FINISH

PLEASE DO NOT FEED HORSE

Photo Finish

ARTISTS
directory

A-1 Master Mold & Casting
Fireman Pony 102
Horse Patrol 102
Adamec, Carol
Running with the Ancestors 5
Alexander, Ellen
Desert Dream Horse 15
Storyteller 81
Alverson, Steve
King Tut's Royal Trotter 7
Anderle, Ty
Dances with Hooves 8

Bagshaw-Tindel, Margarete
Tse-Weeh-Gia-Queejo 25
Bean, Lynn
Fetish Pony 82
Beason, Pat
Muy Caliente 106
Blacksheep, Beverly
I Stand For My Horse 24
Bonny
Russian Folk Tale Pony 54
Bower, Mitzi
Wilderness Roundup 55
Briner, BJ
Snow Pony 14
Brubaker, Kay
Special Gift Horse 7
Bryer, Diana
Southwest Carousel Horse 47

Campbell, Michael
Your Everyday Garden Variety 72
Challenger, JD
As Long As There Is One 9
Chomer, Brett
Turbo Hay Burner 97
Christie, Nevena
Happy Trails 90
Clarke, Joe and Jamie Schene
Kiri Tuhi (Skin Art) 38
Coffaro, Patrick
Fishback Rider 64
Coonts, Bob
Mosaic Appaloosa 100
Creech, Loren
Horsefeathers 80

DeVary, David
Blondes 89
Dieckhoner, Gene
Singing Cowboy Pony 45

Take A Walk On The Wild Side 56

Espinoza, Noel
1910 70
Floral Pony 74
Heavenly Pony 43
Evans, Roger
Wound Up Time On The Range 97

Fallen Heroes Memorial Pony 86

Fudenski, Judy
Snowflake 52

Garcia, Connie
Children of the Garden 50
Milagro Pony 68
Garcia, Letticia
Dog and Pony Show 50
Garcia, Rick
Painted Pony in Garcia Vision 19
Gersch, Wolfgang
Celestial Pony 108
Geryak, John
Saguaro Stallion 77
Granados, Bernie
MadCow Pony 32
Gwinn, Helen
Barnyard Pony 57
Cavern Pony 105

Higgins, Sharon
Cowboy Working Horse 88
Race Horse 93
Holman, Laurie
At Work and At Play 93
Tropical Reef Horse 63
Hood, Rance
War Pony 23
Hoover, Annetta
Rio Grande 73
Hornbuckle, Marianne
Night Pony 72
Horse, Michael
Many Horses 29
Howell-Sickles, Donna
Horse Apples 11
Hudson, Clarissa
Tlingit Robed Horse 30
Hughes, Janee
Photo Finish 91
Dream Horse 41
Fantastic Fillies 92

Great Expectations 94
Incognito 60
Nutcracker Suite Pony 52
Olympia 7
Run For The Roses 92
USET Horse 85
Hummingbird, Jesse
Love As Strong As A Horse 32
Hunter, Michael & Lorien Cook
Mensajero del Milagros 104

Iron Eyes, Mary
Blue Medicine 34
Isenhour, Natasha
Renewal of Life 38

Jirby, Inger
Lady Ledoux 53
John, David K
The Horse From
The Four Directions 33

Kee, Andersen
The Magician 21
Kimble, Jason
Vi's Violet Vision 47
Kinkopf, Kathleen
Three Ring Circus Pony 39
Knauf, Jim
Rodeo Dreams 87
Knox, Grace
Rockin' Horse 47
Seahorse 61
Yankee Doodle 84
Krouse-Cully, Nancy
Poseidon's Pony 62

LaDell Hayes, Arlene
Jeremy The Fish Horse 62
LaRoche, Carole
Ceremonial War Horse 79
Larsen, Fran
Pony Tales 72
Leard, Skeeter
Life Rides The River 58
Lewis-Scott, Elizabeth
Kitty Cat's Ball 53
Lomayesva, Gregory
Butterfly Horse 27
Lopez, Pola
Maize Mustang 67
Losoya, David
Motorcycle Mustang 98

Lowry, Ginger
Horse Flies 105

MacGraw, Ali
Karuna 14
Machado, Carlos
Gladiator 7
MacPherson, Kevin
Paint by Numbers 51
Magener, Ilsa
Sky of Enchantment 44
Marquez, Noel
El Rancho Grande 69
Martin, David
Iron Horse 96
Mattson, Gerri
Five Card Stud 99
Wildfire 75
Mattson, Rich
Horse Power To Burn 95
Menchego, Art
The Swiftness of an Eagle
and The Strength of a Bear 25
Miller, Bill
Ghost Horse 22
Monfils, Georges
Unity 77
Montoya, Martin
One Horse Power 96
Montoya, Roger
Caballo Brillante 66
Moore-Craig, Narca
Horsefeathers 39
Morawski, Kathy
Quarterhorse 84
Morper, Daniel
Tracker 11
Morrow, Kathy
Give Me Wings 83
Horse Feathers 81
Musil, Lori
CowPony 56
USDA: Ladies Choice 88
Year of the Horse 59

Nakamura, Joel
I Dreamed I Was A Blue Horse 37
Kokopelli Pony 48
Thunderbird Suite 10
Namingha, Arlo
Pueblo Pony 30
Navaro, Luis
Running Free 93
Nelson, Benjamin
When They Ran With Freedom 34
Nelson, Bonnie
Horse 'n Buggy 105

Newman, Dave
Hiway Roller 97
Nieto, John
Trailblazer 107
NoiseCat, Ed
Night Flight 30

Ortiz, Virgil
Willing 31

Peacock, Cal
Reunion of the Family of Man 104
Pena, Amado
Caballo-Scape Con Estrellitas 24

Quimby, Barbara
Navajo Blanket Pony 103

Rabbit, Bill
Earth, Wind & Fire 12
Raynes, Jen
By The Dawn's Early Light 107
Red Star, Kevin
Crow Indian War Pony 25
Renk-Mayer, Patrisha
Zorse 42
Rivera, Robert
Anasazi Spirit Horse 78
Robles, Julian
Homage to Degas 18
Romero, Virginia
Caballo Santo 65
Rooks, Patti
Wild Women of the West 89

Sabatino, Chuck
Pueblo Expressions 78
Sago, Warren
Apache 26
Sakiestewa, Ramona
Lowrider 33
Salas, Manuel
Mesoqua Pony 68
Sandoval, Ed
Sacred Heart 66
Schlies, Dianne
Jackson's Jazz 3
Raggedy Rann 103
Scripps, Suzanne
Crows Alight 57
Selden, Lee
Desert Misty 73
Sokoloff, Ellen
Rte 66 Horse 10
Strait, Anne
Caballo de Ojos 106

Strongbow, Dyanne
Lightning Bolt Colt 36
Sweet, Mary
Hokusai's Great Wave Horse 17
Sykes, Rhiannon
Out of Africa 6

Tapia, Luis
Horsepower 96
Tapia, Tom
Tewa Horse 32
Tavlos
It's All Greek To Me 40
Spirit War Pony 79
Thomas-Simpson, Penny
Apple-oosa 100
Tivens, Debra
Opera Warrior Horse 15
Townsend, Storm
Sun Magic 15
Toya, George
Horse of the Rising Sun 28
Tubinaghtewa, Buddy
Grandfather's Journey 22
Tubinaghtewa, Buddy
Indian Summer 35

Vanlandingham, Lynn
Lighthorse 71
Vigil, Frederico
Sabanilla Bella 68
Von Eckhardt, Dorothea
The End Of The Rainbow 40

Wang, David
Hunting 6
Waldrum, Harold Joe
Stabat Mater 101
Wells-Bailey, Wendy
Skyrider 42
Wiggins, Kim
Jazz on a Hot Tin Roof 46
Wolfe, Bassel
Native Bred Pony 75
Wyatt, Patti
On Common Ground 101

Yellowman.
When We Were As One 13
York, Star Liana
Georgia On My Mind 20
Go Van Gogh 18
Medicine Pony 80
Silver Lining 43
Youth of America
Children's Prayer Pony 49

Dear Collector,

While searching for a photographer capable of capturing the magical beauty of the Painted Ponies, we were introduced to Jean-Louis Husson and his business, Feathertech Photography. We soon discovered that he is not only an exceptional photographer, he has a keen eye for design and a superb sense of graphic style. It was our pleasure to work with him on the design and layout of the Collector's Edition, a book that is an art experience in its own right.

Rod Barker
President/Executive Director
The Trail of Painted Ponies

Acknowledgements

In the cowboy heyday, when cattle were rounded up on the ranges in Texas and driven north to the Kansas markets, the average trail herd of fifteen hundred steers was handled by a crew of about ten cowboys. The ratio of Painted Ponies to people who have worked on The Trail of Painted Ponies is about the same. Since this project was first conceived in 2000, it has always been a handful of hardworking individuals who have helped transform an inspired idea into the thriving business that has brought joy to so many people. To all who have ridden with us, I would like to extend a hearty thank you, with a special nod to Ken Kim of Westland Giftware; Ita Golzman of King Features; Hakim, Muhammad and Ibrahim Chishti of IMC Universe; Don Barliant of Barbara's Bestsellers; and our current crew: Cindy Sutton, Myrna Marchese, and Kelly Burke.

For most people, The Trail of Painted Ponies has been experienced through images, which has put a special importance on photography. Over the course of the project, no fewer than eight different photographers have lent the talent that is displayed on the preceding pages, and our appreciation goes out to: Eduardo Fuss, Marty Snortum, Jean-Louis Husson, Bill Davis, Don Bell and Marv Shockley.

I have come to believe that every successful creative endeavor is backed by a muse: someone who whispers in your ear, encouraging you to think bigger and more creatively and to believe in a world of unlimited possibilities. Under the best of circumstances, that muse is also a working partner who stands beside you day-by-day, not only sharing the vision but tending the details that convert what is imagined into reality. For me, and for the Collectors Edition of The Trail of Painted Ponies, that muse has been Karlynn Keyes.

Last but hardly least, I would like to thank the collectors who have purchased Painted Ponies, large and small; the businesses who have supported the project through sponsorships; the museums who have recognized the enduring value of the artwork by including Painted Ponies in their collections; and the fine retailers who represent us around the country.

Happy Trails to All,

Rod Barker
President/Executive Director
The Trail of Painted Ponies

With the Collectors Edition we have organized and selected photographs of those Painted Ponies that we feel best represent the diversity of the project, and that have elicited a positive response from collectors. As such, not all of the Ponies that have been painted are pictured. Below you will find a list of artists who also painted Ponies, and we encourage you to view their work on our website: **www.TrailofPaintedPonies.com**

Alford, Jim
Antuna, Rebecca
Auld, Misty Lyn
Axton, John
Azbell, Charles
Baker, Ron
Beatteay, Cindy
Best, Paula
Blake, Bambi
Bradley, David
Brown, Stacy
Burke, LD
Calles. Rosa Marie
Chelonis, Valerie
Christensen, Peggy
Coffin, Doug
Crabb, Bill
Dixon, Bill
Dowdall, Mike & Stewarwald, Joy
Dryden, Ashley
Escudero, David
Fleming, Nancy
Garcia, Lydia
Gelinas, Katie
Giali, Andy
Grandjean, Dorothy
Graves, Valerie
Gusterson, Leigh
Hadfield, Julienne
Haskew, Denny
Hoback, Priscilla
Hyde, Doug

Jamison, Tracy
Jimenez, Luis, Adan & Orio
Kaminski, Marcia
Kimball, Spencer
Kimura, Eugene
Lack, Del
Lemons, Larry
Levy, Ben
Lewis, Lynne
Lopez, Peter
McGarrell, James
Miles, Gino
Mitchell Edwards, Jackie
Nordwall, Raymond
Norman, Judy
Nowlin, BC
Olguin, Ron
Overhulser, Kevin
Orr, Chrissie
Palma, Israel
Pascal
Peterson, Dorothy
Picavet, Christine
Ramirez, Joel
Ransom, Robert
Reyner, Nancy
Ringholz, Amy
Rothermel, David
Ruthling, Ford
Sampson-Files, Cynthia
Saunders, John
Sawyer, Anne
Schenk, Billy
Schoebel, Henry Leo
Selby, Jeanne
Shore, Rick
Slayton, Mona
Slusher, Carla
Smith, Juan Quick-To-See
Smith, Shawn
Tammen, Claudia
Terranova, Melanie
VandenHueval, Michelle
Wagner, Jim
Weese, Susan
Wells, C.J.
Wening, Karen
Whiting, Wayne
Yank, Karen

www.TrailofPaintedPonies.com